Return the Marshes

Gavin Young spent most of his youth in Cornwall and South Wales. He studied modern history at Oxford University and spent two years with a shipping company in Basra, Iraq, before setting out to live in wilder places – first, with the Marsh Arabs in southern Iraq between the Tigris and Euphrates rivers, and then with the obscure people of the plains and mountains of south-western Arabia. From Tunis he joined the *Observer* as a foreign correspondent in 1960 and subsequently covered fifteen wars and revolutions throughout the world. He has also been the *Observer* correspondent in Paris and New York.

Return to the Marshes was Gavin Young's first book and describes his adventures in the 1950s with the Marsh Arabs who inhabit the ancient land of Sumer and Babylon, and what happened when he returned there many years later. It was the basis of a BBC film in 1979. Next, he wrote *Iraq: Land of Two Rivers*, an account of a journey through the historic landscape of Mesopotania, which was published in 1980. *Slow Boats to China* (1981) told of his seven-month journey from Athens to Canton on twenty-three vessels ranging from freighters to dhows and native schooners. He is currently writing an account of a similar ship-hopping adventure from Shanghai, across the South Seas, round Cape Horn and north from the Falkland Islands back to England.

By the same author

Iraq: Land of Two Rivers
Slow Boats to China

Return to the Marshes

Life with the Marsh Arabs of Iraq

GAVIN YOUNG

Illustrations by Salim

Hutchinson
London Melbourne Sydney Auckland Johannesburg

Hutchinson & Co. (Publishers) Ltd

An imprint of the Hutchinson Publishing Group

17–21 Conway Street, London W1P 6JD

Hutchinson Group (Australia) Pty Ltd
30–32 Cremorne Street, Richmond South, Victoria 3121
PO Box 151, Broadway, New South Wales 2007

Hutchinson Group (NZ) Ltd
32–34 View Road, PO Box 40–086, Glenfield, Auckland 10

Hutchinson Group (SA) Pty Ltd
PO Box 337, Bergvlei 2012, South Africa

First published in Great Britain by William Collins & Sons 1977
Published as a Hutchinson Paperback 1983
© Gavin Young 1977, 1983
Illustrations © Hutchinson Publishing Group 1983
Set in Linotron Sabon by Input Typesetting Limited

Printed in Great Britain by The Anchor Press Ltd
and bound by Wm Brendon & Son Ltd,
both of Tiptree, Essex

British Library Cataloguing in Publication Data
Young, Gavin
     Return to the marshes.
     1. Iraq—Description and travel
     I. Title
     915.67'5   DS760.6

ISBN 0 09 154051 8

Contents

Haur as S'adiya

Haur as Saniya

BA

▲ Lagash

El Gharraf

AL

Shatra ●

Warqa ●

Suwaiq ●

AL BU SALIH

M U N T A F I Q

Euphrates

Nasiriya ●

A
JUA

Ur ▲

Suq esh Shiukh ●

AL HASAN

Khamisiya ●

▢	marshes	～ waterways
▢	open water	▲ ancient city
		AL BU BAKHIT tribal names

N

0	10	20	30 mls
0	10	20	30	40	50 kms

This Book is Dedicated to

Ajram bin Haji Hussein, Hasan bin Manati, Amara bin Thugub, Sabaiti, Hasan bin Muhaisin, Sahain bin Kadhim and his sons Warid, Bani and Mohammed, Falih bin Jasim al Fartusi, Nasaif bin Jasim, Chethir al Faraigi and his brothers Sfair and Ahmed, Sayyid Sarwat and all his sons, Jabbar bin Dair, Farhan bin Saghair and his brother Idan, the sons of Yasin bin Adan, and all the others;

and to the Memory of

Sahain's brother Hafadh bin Kadhim, Yasin bin Adan, Haji Yunis of Al Aggar, Jasim bin Faris of the Fartus, Falih bin Majid Al Khalifa of the Albu Mohammed;

and to

Wilfred Thesiger who first took me to the Marshes;

and to

H. E. Sayyid Tariq Aziz who made it possible for me to go back to them

Author's Note

It is nearly thirty years since Wilfred Thesiger, the European who 'discovered' the Marshes, left them for the last time. It is exactly thirty years since the late Gavin Maxwell spent some weeks there in 1956. Both of them wrote books about their experiences. This book tries to describe what happened next; how changes in Iraq have affected the Marsh Arabs who live in this most beautiful region, both collectively and, in some instances, individually.

I spent a good deal of time in the Marshes in the 1950s; and since 1973 – after a gap of nearly twenty years – I have been back there several times, travelling, as before, in canoes and living with the Marsh people as they live. So this is primarily a personal book; I feel it to be a kind of memorial to my Marsh Arab friends.

I am not a scholar or a specialist. I am not a professional historian, any more than I am an anthropologist, or ornithologist, or any other -ist. But there are chapters of history here too, going back far beyond the battles of the British and Turks, the coming of Islam, the invasions of the Greeks, Persians, Mongols, Medes, Assyrians and the rest, to the time of Ancient Sumer – and even to the beginning of the world. So I am deeply indebted to Dr Edmond Sollberger, Keeper of the Western Asiatic Antiquities Department of the British Museum, for checking my chapter on Sumer and Gilgamesh, for his advice, and for his permission to take photographs in the Museum. I am equally indebted to Professor Charles Beckenham of the London School of Oriental and African Studies for his eagle-eyed perusal of my chapter on the coming of Islam. I owe much to Dr Fuad Safar of the Iraqi Directorate-General of Antiquities in Baghdad for his assistance and advice, and to the staff of Baghdad's superb Iraq Museum for their courtesy.

I also wish to thank Brigadier Stephen Longrigg for taking time to tell me what it was like to be in Mesopotamia in the days immediately after World War I; he was a distinguished member of the British administration of those days. His historical books on Iraq remain invaluable and irreplaceable. I am very grateful, too, to Mrs S. E. Hedgcock for recalling for me her happy days in the Amara area where her late husband was Political Officer in the early 1920s. She remembers with affection the people about whom they wrote – using the pen-name 'Fulanain', and initially for *Blackwood's Magazine* – in the vivid stories that were eventually gathered together in their book *Haji Rikkan: Marsh Arab*.

In transliterating Arabic into English I have tried to make things easy. I have dropped, for instance, the Arabic letter *ain*(') completely. I often use the word 'Madan' for 'Marsh Arabs' because that is what they call themselves. I use it without explaining what it means for the good reason that they themselves have not the faintest idea how the name originated, and because, despite the fact that the great Arab traveller of the fourteenth century, Ibn Battuta, mentions the term Madan, neither he nor anyone since that early time has discovered its meaning.

Mr Naji Al-Hadithi encouraged me with the book; and without the indefatigable assistance of Miss Gritta Weil I doubt if it would have been ready on time. Nor could I possibly have written it if Mr Donald Trelford, the Editor of *The Observer*, had not most kindly agreed to give me the time off in which to do so.

On the Brink

Now it seems to me that I have known the Marsh Arabs of southern Iraq all my life, yet six weeks before meeting them I was hardly aware of their existence. That first meeting took place in the Marshes on a sunny day in 1952, but I had not meant to go there at all. My aching ambition at the time – it was intense and, I thought, irreversible – was to ride a camel across Arabia from the Gulf to the Red Sea.

I was learning Arabic. I had plunged into the writings of famous desert adventurers, and had already snapped up all of T. E. Lawrence, Bertram Thomas and Gertrude Bell, some of H. St John Philby and much of Charles Doughty. I was determined to follow their example at any risk. So when Wilfred Thesiger, who is certainly the last of the great Arabian travellers, came to Basra where I lived and worked in a shipping company, I made sure I met him. I wangled a lunch date from the British Consul and over the meal confidently told Thesiger of my Arabian dream; I was quite sure that such a man would be completely sympathetic to my ambition and offer nothing but encouragement. I was rudely rebuffed. To my intense surprise and utter dismay, Thesiger suggested forgetting the camel.

'You'll never get a visa to enter Saudi Arabia,' he said, flatly.' 'So that's that.'

I had completely forgotten – if I had even noticed – that some political dispute involving Britain and Saudi Arabia had set, for the time being at least, an unbridgeable diplomatic chasm between myself and my Arabian camel. The dishes on the consul's table became a blur; the chilling vision I had been fighting off for months, that of myself writing out bills of lading in a shipping office for the next thirty years, settled on me like a shroud; I felt the weight of my dead dream plummeting to the pit of my stomach to join the consul's undercooked suet-pudding. This, surely, was the end of my ambition. But suddenly Thesiger, who had been about to leave the room, paused in the doorway. 'As an alternative,' he said, in his solemn voice, 'you might consider having a look at the Marshes. I am going up there tomorrow morning, but I shall be back here in six weeks' time for a bath. I could take you up then if you can get some time off from your office.'

At this point I think it is time to say a few words more about this remarkable and incomparable man. Wilfred Thesiger was then in his early forties, but then, as now, there was a timeless quality about him. He was born in Addis Ababa, where his father was the British Minister, and had had an Ethiopian foster-mother. Since then he had explored the remoter parts of the Near and Middle East from the wild Danakil country of Abyssinia to the Hindu Kush, the Karakorams and Nuristan. He had accompanied the Kashgai on their annual migration across the plains of Iran; he had travelled with mules across northern, mountainous Persia and found, among other things, that he liked and respected the Arab tribes, with their warmth of character and hospitality, a good deal more than the stingey and even churlish Persian hillsmen. I suppose no man alive knows more about tribal Arabs than Wilfred Thesiger. He had already, when I first met him, spent years travelling in the Arabian 'outback', through the humid Tihama coastal plain on the Red Sea, through the high, cool, well-watered valleys of the Asir province in the lower Hejaz range. His towering achievement had been his double passage (across it and back), on foot and camel, of the vast waterless deserts and dunes of the Empty Quarter of Southern Arabia – only traversed by two other non-Arabs, Bertram Thomas and H. St John Philby, both of whom started their life with Arabs in the post-Great War British administration in Iraq.

The man I saw at the consul's table in Basra all those years ago was tall and gaunt with a long, creased, sunburnt face, deep-set, probing eyes and large, sinewy, sunburnt wrists and hands. I found later that he was amazingly strong. He had been a successful light-heavyweight boxer at Oxford – but he had a strength quite different from that of a run-of-the-mill under-graduate bruiser. The Marsh Arabs, who naturally admire physical prowess of any kind, were awed by Thesiger's ability to pursue the wild boars of the region on the saddle-less back of a temperamental Arab mare, with the reins in one hand and unerringly shoot the pigs dead, holding his Rigby ·275 rifle in the other hand like a pistol. Anyone who has tried to aim such a relatively heavy rifle one-handed, let alone fire it accurately, will know what special strength of forearm and shoulder this feat requires.

Thesiger, by this time, had established himself through his unmatchable journeys as the greatest traveller of his time, and possibly any other. Of course, he was aware of this. And although he was by no means an offensive *prima donna*, he had a tart tongue in private for some well-known British Arabists who based pretentious claims to great courage and adven-turousness on relatively easy and riskless journeys. Of one such 'intrepid' traveller, he said scornfully, 'Oh, So-and-So! She's never been anywhere one couldn't go by taxi.' And of another inflated reputation he wrote in a book review, 'What's-'is-name is not so much the last of the Arabian travellers as the first of the Arabian tourists.'

These were harsh criticisms, but reasonable, coming from such an uncompromising and genuine man as Thesiger. He hated the intrusion of cars and taxis into beautiful and un-spoiled areas of the world and steered as far clear of them as possible (you could take a taxi to the edge of the Marshes but from there on firm land ceases to exist). He had – and has – strict standards of conduct for travellers. He believes passion-ately (and taught me to believe) that between outsiders and tribesmen stand natural barriers of colour, language, religion, race, upbringing and so forth that are already formidable enough; that no real understanding of people like Marsh Arabs is possible if you add artificial barriers – canned food, mosquito-netting, campbeds, boiled water. And, of course, it is a crime to press alcohol on tribesmen brought up to scorn it. One might say that he is old-fashioned and he would not deny it. The men whose tradition he followed were Richard Burton, Speke, Mungo Park, Doughty, and Lawrence, to pick random names from a noble list. He travelled – and, I am glad to say, still travels – for love; for the love of remote and beautiful peoples in wild and beautiful corners of the world, and for the serene grandeur of desert, river and mountain regions and the wild animals and birds that inhabit them.

Since 1950 Thesiger had been studying the Marsh Arabs in their mysterious and virtually unknown marsh world sixty miles or so north of Basra, living as nearly as possible as one of them, without any artificial aids to comfort, despite heat, insects and stagnant drinking water. As for me, I had no idea what the Marsh Arabs would be like, although I knew vaguely that they lived in the ancient flatlands of Sumer, where civilization was born between the rivers Tigris and Euphrates. But I was still determined to be an explorer despite my disappointment over the camel; and when Thesiger invited me I did not hesitate. I begged a week's leave from my shipping company and presently I was speeding north, braced in the corner of a ramshackle taxi that careered erratically along the uneven asphalt from Basra to the tiny riverside town near Amara that Thesiger had named as our rendezvous.

After three hours of this 'main road' the taxi swung off it, jolted over a rutted mud track until that frayed out into nothing near a wide water-course, and there rocked to a halt. 'Well, here we are,' said the driver genially, and spat through the window. I saw a slender black canoe a few feet away in the water; it rode there majestically, a king of boats, amazingly long and sleek – thirty-six feet long I discovered later – and very beautiful. Thesiger stood beside it and raised a welcoming hand. Four young Arabs with him, wearing black and white check headcloths bound round with thick head ropes, stepped forward grinning and shook my hand, and two of them took my small bag and shotgun – all I could bring, Thesiger had insisted – and loaded them into the canoe. 'I hope that bag isn't too heavy,' Thesiger said, anxiously. He indicated the Arabs – 'These boys are Marsh Arabs. They'll look after you. Step into the dead centre of the canoe or you'll have it over.' I sat crosslegged and too terrified to move in the flat bottom of this work of art, this wonderful boat, so delicately balanced and so low in the water that it seemed bound to capsize. I tried to take comfort from what I read – that these craft had proved superbly efficient for 5000 years – but the effort failed. By now, two Marsh Arabs had hitched their long shirts round their hips and taken up paddles in the high-curved bow, while the other two crouched with their paddles raised in the stern. 'Let's go,' said Thesiger. The four Arabs dipped their paddles together into the pale brown stream, gave them a quick muscular flick of shoulders and arms, and with a lurch that lapped the water to the lip of the gunwales, we shot away.

This branch of the Tigris – the main river has already flowed down from Armenia – whirls deep and strong between its sharp-edged mud banks, slopping water into irrigation channels at intervals and spilling what is left into the Marshes a few miles further on. It often seems to give little to the surrounding land, which is flat and dry and cracked for much of the year. But, at other times, irrigation with pumps ensures crops of rice, sugar and barley, and then as far as the eye can see wide green swathes cut through the dusty, dun-brown flatness. The land of Sumer outside the Marshes is a monotonous prospect interrupted by isolated figures of long-robed people, a man or two on horseback, many birds, and clusters of cattle. Here and there, a distant clump of trees signals a village strung along one of many water-channels. Otherwise the flatness of Mesopotamia prevails. The houses here are made, Marsh-fashion, out of reeds. But these villagers are tribesmen-cultivators; peasant *fellah*, not Madan (Marsh Arabs) like our canoe-men, though they are experts at handling canoes which are the indispensable transport of the waterways.

The major side-channel we were on, called Wadiya, led us

through low, level land only occasionally varied by willows whose branches scores of black and white pied kingfishers used as springboards for diving after fish. Sometimes we met men cloaked and robed, in canoes like ours but smaller, who murmured to us '*Salaam aleikum*', touching their foreheads with their open palms, as we did in return. The world of my conventional British upbringing, the shipping office, Basra, clubs, motor-cars, and whisky and soda, seemed a million miles away. I glanced back, but by now even the waterside town at which we had recently embarked had vanished into the distance. We had entered a new, perceptibly more tranquil and, to me, magical world. Despite the scattered human figures, this drowsy landscape breathed an extraordinary solitude of peace. Even today, with visible evidence of a more intensive agriculture and the occasional jet aircraft overhead, it unfailingly does so.

So it seemed a long dreamy haul before the first man in the prow said something and pointed ahead. Our canoe-men picked up the stroke and, as we turned a corner, I saw a great reed house – a house like a reed church – on a fork of the waterway. A few men in Arab dress stood by this dramatic structure. 'Here we are,' said Thesiger. 'That is Falih's guest-house,' and the boys deftly steered the canoe alongside the low bank. Falih bin Majid Khalifa was the son of an outstandingly powerful sheikh of the region. Thesiger had stayed with him many times, and Falih had lent him his own war-canoe and canoe-man when he first set out to penetrate the deep, permanent Marsh. Later Falih presented him a brand new war-canoe, specifically and expensively built for him in the Marshes by master-craftsmen – the sleek, beautiful, thoroughbred thing we sat in now. I stood up; the canoe-boys steadied the tremulous boat by gripping grass tufts on the bank; I stepped ashore. I remember – the scene is fixed in my mind like the frozen frame of a film – that a thick-set man with a black and white headcloth and a small black moustache gripped my hand and that he said something to Thesiger and smiled with great warmth. Others followed Falih and took my hand: one or two stooped old men with grey, stubbly beards (one irregularly dyed black), a sallow-faced *sayyid* (one of many venerated men accepted by the Muslims in these parts as descendants of the Prophet Mohammed), some smooth-cheeked youngsters who seemed from their gold-braided cloaks to be specially related to the sheikh, and several muscular and bandoliered retainers with bolt-action rifles who squeezed my hand solemnly and painfully in strong, rough palms. Behind those hovered one or two servants in white robes, and I noted on their darker faces the pronounced Negroid features of ex-slaves. Behind them, several dangerous-looking heavy-set dogs prowled and growled, and two fine chestnut Arab mares stood hobbled and covered with blankets. Thesiger's canoe-men carted my modest bag and my gun in through the high, arched entrance of the guest-house, the curving reed columns of which were turning a mellower honeygold in the slanting afternoon sunlight. 'The Marshes are just over there,' Thesiger said, and I strained my eyes hopefully at the skyline. I saw, not the Marshes, but a vague line of palm trees and the blood-orange disk of the sun sinking into a low evening haze. Yet in the years that followed I came to recognize the new feeling that possessed me at that moment: the exquisite thrust of excitement under the breast-bone, as keen as indigestion, that only tranquil end-of-the-world places – deserts, mountains, seas and these marshes – can induce. I suppose many others feel it, too; I felt it then at Falih's. Today when I pass the place where his house used to be (you can see nothing there now except scrub and a dancing cloud of midges and, if you are lucky, a solitary heron fishing) I am convinced that I can smell the waters of the lagoons in the Marsh's heart, and even think that I can see – although they are much too far away – the waving white plumes of the first giant reed-beds. But at that moment I simply saw that, without any possibility of doubt, I was on the brink of a great adventure.

Of course, Falih's was only the threshold. It took the best part of the next morning to reach the permanent Marsh. First, Falih and his servants provided the unavoidable Arab ritual of breakfast: eggs and jam and flat bread, with small glasses of sugary tea. Then our canoe-men loaded the canoe, and again I stepped gingerly aboard it, squatting on a vividly coloured rug that Falih had ordered to be spread amidships. A crowd of people waved us goodbye, calling 'Come back. Come back soon.'

Falih's heavy figure stood watching us until we turned the next bend in the water-channel and a clump of willows hid him. The monotony of the low, flat land resumed. But we hadn't travelled far before the canoe-boys broke off their desultory conversation to point and chatter. On the right bank ahead I saw another great reed *mudhif* (guest-house) and people, as at Falih's, moving out of its shadowy, arched doorway to watch us approach. There was a difference here for nearly all of them wore dark blue *kefiyahs* (headcloths) instead of the customary black and white check ones. By that sign we could tell that they were *sayyids*, like the sallow-faced man at Falih's. The owner of this guest-house, Sayyid Sarwat, was the most respected of all the *sayyids* in these parts; a man known and loved through all southern Iraq up to Baghdad, even to Kuwait. His prestige was immense – not only among superstitious Marsh Arabs and the ultra-religious; with the sheikhs and government officials of the area, too, his wisdom and probity were unquestioned.

This much Thesiger had told me. And I could see the Sayyid now looming on the shore – and loom is very much the appropriate word. For Sayyid Sarwat is a very large man indeed; six feet tall, broad, thick, and made even more imposing by his black beard, black robes from chin to ankle, and a cavernous, bass voice that at this moment was filling the wide landscape with genial booms of welcome in our direction. On later occasions I always stopped here; it was a place of loving kindness and boundless hospitality, a place to rest and be at ease in after hard days and nights in the Marshes, a place in which to catch up on local gossip; a place of common sense; a good place. But we needed to hurry on: my first visit here had to be short. I still worked for a company with ships to load down in Basra and in a few days I was expected to be aboard them, arguing with German or Dutch First Officers about the stowage of the barley

the company exported. So we exchanged hails with the Sayyid,
pulling our canoe alongside to shake his enormous hand, and
left the great man, thunderously upbraiding us across the water,
his arms raised in mock anger at our refusal to stay to lunch,
dinner, the night, three days, a week. . . .

Presently we were very close to the Marshes. Any minute
now I would see if I had abandoned too lightly that ambition
to take to the great desert with a camel. Our water-course
narrowed perceptibly; a tall palisade of reeds suddenly reared
up and seemed to bar our way. In a moment our channel faded
out completely and messily into a small stretch of water-logged
silt. To prevent us sticking, the boys leapt over the side, their
clothing tucked up round their waists, and, thigh-deep in mud,
began heaving the canoe forward by main force. Not for long.
With a gentle rasping sound, the boat slid off the mud-field and

into wide, clear water like a swan taking gratefully to its true element. The golden reeds shot up around us, closing up behind us like twenty feet high sound-proof screens, shutting out all other worlds. Their dun-coloured waving plumes contracted the sky into one pure blue swathe immediately overhead. Like Alice in Wonderland we had plunged into another world. However insignificant on a map, the Marsh is a world to get lost in: 6000 square miles, give or take a few. Shifting their paddles from one side to the other, the canoe-men threaded our needle-slim prow through a weaving half-tunnel of reed, rush and tangled sedge. I looked over the side and saw water as clear as glass and deep creepers, and flickering fish. 'You're there,' said Thesiger. 'This is the Marsh.' And the canoe-boy kneeling immediately behind me tapped me on the shoulder and excitedly echoed Thesiger, '*Hadha el Hor*'.

This was the Marsh all right. The impressions of the next few days of this visit took hold of me as relentlessly as the marsh creepers that grapple those millions upon millions of reeds. Sometimes we burst out of the reed-forests into dazzling sun-lit lagoons so vast that their blue mirror-surfaces joined the sky uninterrupted by any solid skyline. We saw Marshmen in the prows of their canoes of immemorial design, bending against the curve of a reed punt-pole, or poised with long five-pronged fishing-spears like javelin-throwers on an ancient frieze, bracing strong bodies the colour of butterscotch. Others seemed dressed for the warpath; clutching Lee-Enfield rifles and festooned with cartridge belts, they paddled past strongly and fast in silence with a grim, preoccupied air. I saw men and boys leaping in and out of canoes, even in deep water, with an agility that seemed almost incredible until I remembered that they had four or five thousand years of practice behind them.

We stayed in island-built Marsh villages, where you need a canoe to go from one shaggy reed house to another and the houses sit on the water, as Gavin Maxwell described them so accurately, 'like a fleet of lit boats at anchor in a calm sea'. Through the open doorways of these humble replicas of Falih's magnificent guest-house I saw men or women sitting round fires that illuminated their faces orange-red, like figures in a seventeenth-century painting. I longed to touch them and talk to them and in some way share their lives. There and then I forgot about camels and deserts.

The natural beauty of the place was hypnotic. Black and white pied kingfishers dived for their prey all around us, clusters of storks arced high above, snow-white flotillas of stately pelicans fished the lagoons; there was always at least one eagle in the sky. The reeds we passed through trembled or crashed with hidden wildlife: otters, herons, coot, warblers, gaudy purple gallinule, pygmy cormorants, huge and dangerous wild pigs. And often, out of some apparently deserted reed-jungle, a full-throated human voice soared into the silence – a young Marsh Arab singing a love-song as he harvested the rushes. The canoe-boys might stop paddling to listen and they grunted appreciatively if the voice was good. They were moist-eyed and soulful only when they themselves were singing. I found the sound of those unselfconscious singers invariably moving. The young voice throbbed and choked with sadness, real or feigned. In that great solitude, where the men of Ur once poled their canoes and where 'in the beginning', according to Sumerian legend, Marduk, the great God, built a reed platform on the surface of the waters and thus created the world, the effect is one of unquenchable and universal yearning.

2. In the Beginning

'Reed-house, reed-house! Wall, O Wall, harken reed-house . . . O man of Shuruppak, son of Ubaru-Tutu; tear down your home and build a boat. . . .'

The Epic of Gilgamesh
The Story of the Flood (from 3000 BC)

Before Men came, Mesopotamia was a lifeless swirl of air, water and mist. At least, that is what legend says, and we do not know any better. Up to the third millennium BC, the history of Ancient Iraq is elusive. Did civilized Man appear there six thousand years ago, or seven thousand? That far back in time, even the experts allow themselves a few centuries of doubt this way or that. The Marsh Arabs, for their part, know next to nothing about their remote ancestors, and so are no help.

One day I asked an elderly Marsh Arab how far back he could trace his antecedents as marsh-dwellers, and he replied, 'Really, I don't know how long we have been here. I think perhaps ten generations ago my tribe moved here from the dry land round about. I am not an educated man who would know such things, but I don't think there was anything here before that except the birds and the beasts.' Yet, as he spoke, we sat in the heart of a region in which human life had existed since 3500 BC and very probably many centuries earlier than that. An aura of infinity hangs over these sometimes exhilaratingly beautiful Marshes, these sometimes gloomy and disturbing 6000 square miles of water and reed. And why should it

surprise, that intimation of infinity? Is it a little matter that five thousand years ago the kings of Ur of the Chaldees gazed at the curved reed houses that we can gaze at and visit today? That we can travel today in the royal gondolas of Sumer and Babylonia?

A mass of texts excavated from numerous Sumerian sites during the last hundred years shows just how early in history human beings worked and frolicked in Mesopotamia. The Sumerians were the first literate inhabitants of southern Iraq. They invented writing and beyond argument must be counted among the most gifted people the world has ever seen. According to some scholars, the Sumerians arrived from the north and east of Iraq sometime before 3000 BC. Others maintain that they were a mixture of new arrivals from outside Iraq and already settled indigenous peoples of the south with their own civilization in embryo already burgeoning there. The second lot of scholars seem to be in the ascendant. But wherever they did or did not come from, the Sumerians created in Mesopotamia a civilization of a grandeur unsurpassed by Egypt. The Nile Valley and the plains of Greece left no treasures more dazzling than those the archaeologists have dug up in Mesopotamian cities like Ur, Uruk, Nippur, Assur and Babylon.

Sumer was about the size of Belgium (about 10,000 square miles), a long, rather narrow stretch of irrigated land between Baghdad and the Marshes at the head of the Gulf, which was known to Sumerians as 'the Lower Sea' or 'Sea of the Rising Sun'. The numerous Sumerian city-states straggled up to the general area of present-day Baghdad from the city-state of Eridu just south of Ur, which is a short drive from modern Nasiriya. They were large and sophisticated settlements consisting of suburbs, satellite towns, gardens and orchards; one may have encompassed a population of 30,000 to 35,000. These city-states, with their temples and defensive walls and dykes, were tightly organized by large civil services under the eagle eyes of high priests. Each city-state was ruled by a king or governor, but he was simply the representative, or vicar, of the gods on earth – and chosen by them – for each state was not only protected but actually owned by a particular god. Ziggurats of the kind still visible at Ur were, like the Tower of Babel (Babylon), attempts to bridge the gap between mortals and the gods above. In the cities on the fringe of the giant reed-beds, writing was born (about 3000 BC) and developed, at first in the form of pictograms, simple drawings scratched on clay with reed stalks, and later as cuneiform impressed on clay tablets baked as hard as stone; hundreds of thousands of these have survived. Most were found relatively recently. The 'heroic age' of archaeology in Mesopotamia began in the nineteenth century with the early diggings of Claudius Rich of the East India Company, and continued gloriously with Sir Henry Layard's successes at Nineveh and the work of Sir Henry Rawlinson, the army officer-philologist who cracked the secret 'code' of the cuneiform texts. The twentieth century has contributed the triumphs of Sir Leonard Woolley, Dr Parrot of France, Sir Max Mallowan and Dr Fuad Safar of the Directorate-General of Antiquities in Baghdad, and of Dr Samuel Noah Kramer of Pennsylvania who re-discovered Sumerian literature (to list only a few illustrious names). At least a quarter of a million tablets have been unearthed – more ancient texts than any other country has disclosed – and the work of discovery still goes on, turning up more and more. There is still much to find. What ruins lie under the waters of the Marshes, for example, or under the silt?

This great civilization took shape in uncomfortable surroundings: on the edge of – and even within – the Marshes, in a flat plain made habitable by the twin rivers Euphrates and Tigris, where summer temperatures soared to 120° and coupled with intense humidity to make breathing, leave alone hard physical effort, a trial. From the wealth of carvings on cylinder-seals and impressions on tablets, from relief carvings on stone vases and bowls, and from breath-taking sculpture, we can have a very good idea of what they looked like, these indefatigable temple-builders, artists, law-givers, cultivators – and the men of the Marshes who stalked wild-fowl in the reed-beds and speared or netted fish. The Sumerians were often potato-faced, stocky with thick necks, big protuberant noses and large, un-usually round eyes – no great beauties, one would say, although their faces show an exuberant strength of character and much humour. After the Sumerians, who were not Semitic whatever else they were, people came from further north who had short, straight noses and heads finer and less round – the Semitic look introduced by the incursions of Akkadian princes from central Iraq. You can see both types of feature (among others) round evening firesides in Marsh houses today. But their owners will not be chattering away in old Sumerian.

The Sumerian language is an unclassified tongue; it has no connection with any other language such as Akkadian (or Assyro-Babylonian), which is a Semitic language related to Hebrew and Arabic. It died out about 2000 BC as a spoken tongue for day-to-day communication. It survived for centuries (such was the strength of Sumerian culture and such the deep respect for it of succeeding 'foreign' conquerors of Southern Mesopotamia like the Babylonians and Assyrians) as the written, academic language of priests and scholars, much as Latin survived in Europe through the Middle Ages. There is no linguistic link therefore with the tongue of the Marsh people of today, who speak Arabic in the Iraqi dialect.

Language apart, I think a Sumerian's shock of recognition would overcome his shock of surprise if, by some magical time-mechanism, I could snatch him from 3000 BC, or even long before that, and plonk him down in a high-prowed Marsh Arab's canoe built, say, in 1976, and moored at the threshold of a reed house completed last week. Relics of *mashhufs* from that distant 'golden age' of Sumer are accurately reflected by the Marshmen's boats today. Sir Leonard Woolley found a two-foot long silver model of a *mashhuf* in the remains of the royal city of Ur, which is only forty miles from the centre of today's permanent marsh. The model is now on show in the exceptionally fine Iraq Museum in Baghdad. Two larger models from Ur, made of bitumen, are displayed in the British Museum in London. Bitumen models crop up throughout the Sumerian period, some only a foot and a half in length, others as much as six feet. These models of the *mashhufs* of the ancient fens seem to have had a religious significance, since they were found inside Sumerian graves and had clearly been made there. They bore miniature cargoes of copper pots and jars containing offerings of food and drink intended either for the hungry dead, or to lure evil spirits aboard the boats which would then shuttle them away to oblivion.

The finely-shaped canoes the Madan use almost as much today as ever before closely resemble those ancient models. All of them, particularly the *taradas* or war-canoes of the sheikhs, are things of a rare, almost animal, grace. The war-canoe Falih bin Majid had built for Wilfred Thesiger in 1951 measured thirty-six feet long, though it was only three and a half feet across at its widest. Its sleek prow swept up to a point five feet above the surface of the water, smooth and black with bitumen. Five thousand years ago, the Sumerians built their boats as they do today. *Mashhufs* and *taradas* are carvel-built out of a mixture of Iraqi mulberry wood and wood imported from Malaysia and Indonesia, with the simplest of tools: a saw, an adze, a drill. When the curving Java-wood ribs have been attached to the

lighter slats of the bottom, that are laid out on the ground like a skeleton, a cross-beam is nailed in to buttress the sides. Detachable floor-boards are slipped in, and a small part of the bows and stern are decked to provide space for two punters or paddlers fore and aft.

The Sumerians used the same method of water-proofing that you can watch Marsh Arab craftsmen applying today, smearing the delicate wooden hulls with a skin of the pitch that bubbled out of the ground – and bubbles still – at Hit and Ramadi. (The Sumerians also used the bitumen for water-proofing drains, and as mortar in brickwork.) Every year the bitumen skin is scraped off and a fresh coat put on with a sort of rolling-pin.

Given the identical nature of the landscape then and now, why should one wonder that Sumerian legends were largely fixed into settings resembling southern Iraq today: rivers, reeds, marshes, date-palms? The Sumerian and Babylonian tradition of the Creation fits perfectly into the grey-green flatness at the head of the Gulf. 'If we stand on a misty morning near the present Iraqi sea-shore, at the mouth of the Shatt al Arab,' wrote a recent historian of early Iraq who obviously knows what it looks like, 'what do we see? Low banks of clouds hang over the horizon; large pools of sweet water seeping from underground or left over from the river floods mingle freely with the salty waters of the Gulf; of the low mud-flats which normally form the landscape no more than a few feet are visible; all around us sea, sky and earth are mixed in a nebulous, watery chaos.' This, he points out, is how the peoples of this ancient region must have envisaged the beginning of the world. In fact, we know that they did so from an early masterpiece of literature. An epic poem composed by the Babylonians and transcribed onto seven tablets about 2000 BC sets out a detailed account of the Creation legend, an account probably handed down from the even earlier Sumerian times. The creation of the world, these tablets proclaim, was the outcome of a desperate struggle between various combinations of turbulent gods; a titanic confrontation between Good and Evil, Order and Chaos.

Entitled *Enuma Elish* from its opening sentence, 'When on high (the heaven had not been named. . .)', the poem describes the time when nothing at all had been created – 'no reed-hut had been matted, no marsh land had appeared. . . .' Only Apsu (the sweet waters), Tiamat (the salt waters) and Mimmu (the clouds) 'co-mingled their waters as a single body'. Confusion, watery and melancholy, prevailed. A divine miracle was required, and presently it came. The Babylonians credit their patron-god, Marduk – Enlil to the Sumerians – with the creation of Order, the world and human beings. Mounting his storm-chariot and armed with flood-storm and lightning, Marduk/Enlil smote and routed the forces of Chaos, a motley army of dragons and monstrous serpents. He proceeded to create a new sky and to fix the sun, moon and stars in proper courses.

Then he went on to make the world. 'He built a reed platform on the surface of the waters, then created dust and poured it around the platform' – and this, briefly stated, is how today's Madan create the artificial islands on which they site their reed houses. Finally, Marduk/Enlil made sure there would be someone about to give credit where it was due. He said: 'I will establish a savage, "man" shall be his name. Verily, savage-man I will create. He shall be charged with the service of the gods, That they might be at ease!' And so Man came into the world.

The Sumerians and Babylonians, though grateful for the gift of life, were all aware of the black side to the green well-watered land Marduk/Enlil had made. Floods washed down city walls and destroyed crops and cattle. The blessed rivers, Tigris and Euphrates, by grace of which Iraq has survived, could break their banks and bring disaster. Winter rains, sandstorms, summer heat and drought were all regular threats to prosperity, or even to survival. So, for nearly two thousand years, the canny and uneasy priests of Babylon recited *Enuma Elish* on the fourth day of their New Year Festival – a scrupulous propitiation of the great god Marduk and a reasonable expression of thanks, but equally a sign that the Babylonians were by no means certain that the cosmic contest between Order and Chaos had been decided once and for all.

So much for the *legend* of the creation of the Sumerian and Babylonian world – a world restricted to Mesopotamia and the immediately adjacent regions, with Babylon as its capital for the Babylonians and Nippur for the Sumerians. What of the reality?

Here controversy sets in among the academics. Up to recent years, scholars believed that until the biblical era, the sea – or, more precisely, the Gulf – covered what is now land, all the way up to Ur and to some point between Qurna and the modern town of Amara. Doubts about the bulge of sea up the Qurna-Amara axis arose when engineers putting down wells in that area failed to find any marine shells that the sea would have brought with it and, on receding, have left behind. Questing geologists had discovered such shells in the Ur region and the great city undoubtedly stood near the sea-shore. This theory is supported by a German, Werner Nützel, who has also presented a new and startling picture of the rise and fall of the ancient oceans. At the time of the coldest Ice Age which lasted (roughly) from 14,000 to 13,000 BC, Nützel maintains, the enormous extension of the glacial regions of the earth sucked up enough water from the oceans to cause the world's sea-levels to fall about a 110 meters below the present. The Gulf is only a 100 meters at its deepest. Thus, he goes on, the Gulf must have been a dry depression during this period, only attaining its present form in the fifth millennium after the melting process has raised the level once more. But Nützel says that in about 3500 BC an extra warm Warm Age temporarily raised the water-level still higher, to about three meters above today's level. Such swollen waters would have meant a rush of flood-bores north-westwards, breaching or overwhelming walls, irrigation ditches and dykes and outflanking the sea-shore cities of Uruk and Ur. It would have caused major damage to the reed-houses of the peasant and marsh communities, destroying their crops and cattle and even drowning the marshmen themselves: it would have been an unforgettable disaster. It would explain why the Sumerians and Babylonians wrote obsessively of a Great Flood in their ancient texts. The biblical flood story derives from those Sumerian obsessions.

The grubbiest urchin herding buffaloes in the southern Iraq of those ancient times must have known, loved and feared the thrilling story of the Deluge. It must have been told and re-told in countless reed houses by generations of mothers to generations of sons and daughters – this legend of the sudden explosion of anger in heaven and the sending of great waters to exterminate Mankind. Of course, the story of Man's hair's-breadth escape with its built-in and menacing implications – 'It could happen again!' – spread throughout the Near East. When the Third Dynasty of Ur (*c.* 2110–2010 BC) fell to the onslaughts of eastern invaders, one of the refugees from the city was Abraham, who decamped, lock, stock and barrel, to Palestine. Besides his family, servants, goods and animals, he took with him the brilliant literary traditions and glowing legends of Sumer. And among these was the story of the flood that would be seized on by the authors of the biblical account of it that we all know.

The Flood story was certainly passed down by word of mouth to generations of Sumerians, Babylonians and Assyrians. It contributed a glowing chapter to the crowning glory of Sumerian literature – a magnificent epic poem in twelve cantos known as *The Epic of Gilgamesh*. A mixture of adventure, morality and tragedy, *The Epic of Gilgamesh* has been described as 'the finest surviving epic poem from any period until Homer's *Iliad*.' It is fifteen hundred years older than Homer, first written down early in the second millennium on clay tablets in cuneiform, the oldest of all scripts, although familiar to Sumerians many centuries before that. (One of the greatest Sumerologists of our day, Dr Samuel Noah Kramer of Pennsylvania, has shown through his collection of translations of Sumerian texts that the accounts of the Flood in it were certainly known as far back as 3000 BC).

Gilgamesh was a real king of the Sumerian city-state of Uruk (north-west of Ur and now known as Warka) and lived about 2700 BC. In life a great and just judge and a builder of temples, in death he became a legend, two parts god and one part man. The Gilgamesh *Epic*, in part, describes his restless quest for the secret of eternal life; a quest which takes him, after many adventures and dangers, to the presence of Uta-napishtim, the builder of the 'ark' and survivor of the Flood, to whom the gods have given immortality as compensation for his tribulations during the Deluge. Uta-napishtim now lives 'at the mouth of the rivers' in the idyllic land of Dilmun, where, the early Sumerians thought, 'when the world was young . . . the croak of the raven was not heard, the bird of death did not utter the cry of death, the lion did not devour, the wolf did not rend the lamb, the dove did not mourn, there was no widow, no sickness, no old age, no lamentation'. Uta-napishtim tells Gilgamesh the secret of a unique plant that can give him immortality. Gilgamesh eventually finds it at the bottom of the sea but, bearing it home, he stops to bathe in a stream and a serpent steals out of the water and carries the plant away. At last and in despair, Gilgamesh accepts his mortal fate.

Earlier, however, during their conversation old Uta-napishtim has related to Gilgamesh his eye-witness story of the flood.

Enlil, 'father of the gods', was responsible for it. He had worked the miracle of Creation by making a reed island on the surface of the water and placing Man on it. Later, he convinced the other gods that they should send a flood to obliterate all animal life. It was an astounding thing to do. Nothing resembling a reasonable justification for such a terrible act is to be found in the ancient texts – nothing, that is, except a Babylonian suggestion that 'the population of the earth became so numerous and noisy that Enlil was upset by their uproar'. At any rate, only the god Enki, god of wisdom and peace, disagreed with the majority decision – 'Why deprive ourselves,' he argued, 'of our human servants and worshippers?' What possible sense could there be, in fact, in the decision of a histrionic company of gods to kill off once and for all a unique and respectful human audience – one which could easily have been punished adequately by famine, say, or a plague of lions?

The assembly's decision, however, was unchallengeable. Enki could do nothing to prevent the flood taking place. All he could do was to warn one man that a flood was coming so as to give him time to build a boat; this would at least ensure the survival of man- and animal-kind. Because the code of the gods precluded him from divulging celestial secrets directly to a mortal's ear, Enki whispered his warning to the wall of Uta-napishtim's reed hut: 'Reed-house, reed-house! Wall, O wall, harken reed-house, wall reflect; O man of Shuruppak, son of Ubara-Tutu; tear down your house and build a boat, abandon possessions and look for life . . . take up into the boat the seed of all living creatures.' So Uta-napishtim of the city of Shuruppak (it was found by archaeologists about forty miles north-west of Ur)

built his 'ark' and embarked his family, and 'the beasts of the
field both wild and tame, and all the craftsmen'. Soon, according
to the early Sumerian account: 'The mighty storm-winds, all of
them together, they rushed. . . . And the storm-winds tossed the
huge boat on the great waters.'

Mankind was decimated. Eventually, but too late for the
wretched men and animals already drowned, the gods were
appalled by what they had done and they caused the flood to
abate. The great boat came to rest on Mount Nisir, now thought
to be Pir Omar Gudrun, east of the Tigris in the Lesser Zab
river basin. Here, Uta-napishtim hopefully released a dove
which flew around, found no land to alight on and returned to
the boat. The same thing happened when Uta-napishtim released a swallow. Then, however, a raven left the boat with its
complement of animals and anxious humans, and was never
seen again; it had found land. The waters rapidly receded; and
Uta-napishtim promptly sacrificed to the gods who had done
their best to annihilate him.

Enlil, at first unrepentant, was furious that any mortal had
escaped, but even he was soon convinced that the Deluge had
been a serious error of judgement. As old Uta-napishtim told
Gilgamesh much later, 'Enlil went up into the boat, he took me
by the hand and my wife and made us enter the boat and kneel
down on either side, he standing between us. He touched our
foreheads to bless us saying, "In time past Uta-napishtim was
a mortal man; henceforth he and his wife shall be equal like to
us gods; in the distance afar at the mouth of the rivers." '

The Biblical Flood stories end reassuringly with the appearance of the rainbow. The Sumerian and Babylonian accounts
contain no such divine guarantees against another Deluge. It is
true that Uta-napishtim's account, in *The Epic of Gilgamesh*,
of the god's profound remorse contains some comfort for man.
Yet the *Epic* ends somberly. For even Gilgamesh – for generations the legendary king-hero of southern Iraq – was doomed
to see immortality snatched from him by a serpent. Even he
was obliged to recognize that the lot of man is Death.

3 From Sumer to Islam

Apart from the Great Deluge, ancient peoples of Iraq had to put up with an endless succession of smaller floods with as much stoicism as they put up with disease. Dr Fuad Safar, a distinguished Iraqi Sumerologist, says that in the old, old days the waters of the Tigris regularly and very disruptively flooded the areas north, north-east, south-east and south of the present-day city of Amara. Sumer proper and most of its population occupied what is now called Muntafiq – that is, the area that runs from modern Nasiriya, Suq-esh-Shiukh and Shatra up to Babylon. No two experts agree completely on the exact form the Marshes took then. Even the former courses of the two great rivers on which all streams, irrigation canals and marshes in the south depend, are uncertain. Now, of course, rising high in Armenia, they meet at Qurna and flow together down the Shatt al Arab waterway to the sea; on the map they look like an enormous tuning fork. But it is perfectly possible that once upon a time the Euphrates flowed south from Samawa, and ran separately to the sea.

Through an eagle's eyes the lands of Sumer resemble a bad case of chicken-pox. Literally thousands of hillocks (*tels*) and strange mounds (*ishans*) dot the landscape, marking the sites of as many hamlets, villages and towns. They sit there, mysterious and inscrutable today; so far unnamed and unidentified, awaiting the arrival of the excavators. Many of these antique mounds straggle through the Marshes. One of them, at Abu Shadhr in the central Marshes, I often visit. It is about 300 feet long, 200 feet wide and some 10 feet above water when it is at an average height. Today, Abu Shadhr is inhabited by the Beit Nasrullah tribe of Marsh Arabs, their buffaloes and some cattle. There is something creepy about it.

The only time I have seen buffaloes behave in anything but a peaceful way was at Abu Shadhr a year ago. One of the canoe-men had a friend among the Beit Nasrullah and we drew the *tarada* up on the shore of the island, shook hands with our hosts and went for a stroll across this strange, large excrescence of earth. There was not much to see. A considerable number of water-buffaloes were chewing fodder in the centre of Abu Shadhr but that was nothing out of the ordinary.

Then all of a sudden, an amazing thing happened. The buffaloes scrambled to their feet with extraordinary agility, groaning wildly, and lowered their horns at us. Like fighting bulls, they began to paw up the dust with their hooves, looking not simply alarmed but distinctly aggressive as well. They were clearly about to charge.

'Look out!' yelled Jabbar, the youngest and liveliest of my companions. He instantly snatched up a large stone and a short length of wood lying by. The others did likewise and darted foward hurling the stones and shouting frantically. Furiously snorting, the buffaloes turned away from this unexpectedly brisk attack and cantered to the other end of the island where they stood blowing nervously through their nostrils and looking aggrieved. But it was curious.

'What made them do that?' I asked. No one could tell.

'If that had happened years ago,' Farhan, another canoe-boy, laughed, 'we would have said it was the *tantals*, the sprites and spirits that our grandfathers and fathers believed lived in these islands.'

These *tantals*, of which many stories are told round the night fires, were also said to guard mysterious treasure buried on an island which they hid with magic from the eyes of men. Local tribesmen used to say that gold was buried here, but no gold has actually been dug up, as far as I know. On the other hand, someone showed Thesiger an old seal and a piece of lead sheeting with what he was told were Phoenician characters scratched on it. John George Taylor, who was British Vice-Consul at Basra in 1853, had explored bits of 'the Chaldean Lake' (as he called the Marshes) and he too found rolls of sheet lead in sepulchral jars with prayers and invocations scratched on them with *stili*. The experts now say all these scratchings are from the sixth century AD and in the Mandean language of the Sabaeans, an ancient sect which still inhabits the region. If they were there thirteen hundred years ago, these island-mounds – though not the seals – were very likely there in pre-Islamic times, even in the time of Sumer. Some of them are solid, of the solidity of earth, not rock, and very high. Thesiger wrote about seeing a bare, black mound standing 30 feet above the reeds. To the Marsh people it is *Ishan Waqif* or Standing Island, and they take it for the site of a long-forgotten city. Later Thesiger saw a mound they call Azizah which he estimated as 50 feet high. Both of these colossal mounds are in Suaid country, towards the Persian border east of Amara. You find bits of pottery there, too, some unglazed, some sky-blue. Now and again a Marsh Arab picks up a square, flat brick with what looks like cuneiform symbols on it, and sometimes crumbling masonry, glazed dark green. Some of these things may be relatively modern, perhaps Islamic. But other things, and things still buried and unseen, could easily be very old indeed.

Life was good there in those remote times. The green, well-watered gardens, orchards and seemingly endless date-forests of Sumer; the gloriously intricate cobweb of canals and dykes that made Mesopotamia the granary of the Near East; prosperous farmers with their thousands upon thousands of sheep and cattle; singing boatmen in the giant reeds fishing and hunting undisturbed: such was the golden prospect when southern Iraq was as young. A paradise – to be lost later through conflict and neglect.

The Sumerians, it is thought, brought the ancestors of the Iraqi water-buffalo from India sometime before 3000 BC. Today, as then, you see their black hulk-bodies huddled on the

small rounded platforms on every island house of the Madan, and often beside the houses of land-based cultivators, too. Of course they are as tame as the Marshmen's cows, but their vast bulk and the heavy swing of the gnarled bosses of their thick, wide horns make you wonder at first sight how they are going to take to you. Especially as you jump from a canoe onto the narrow threshold of a Marsh house where they will often be standing or lying close-packed enough to make you bump them as you pass. There is no need to worry. Despite their grotesque appearance, the great pampered creatures seem to have hardly enough energy to chew the fodder in their ruminant mouths after the centuries of selfless attention lavished on them by generation after generation of Marsh Arabs. The Madan seldom slaughter them for meat; they are prized only for their milk and dung. Dried into thin pats like small rounds of unleavened bread, the manure is the best fuel for the Marsh people's long-burning household fires and also the hard-sealing cement-like substance most easily and cheaply available.

Buffalo milk is drunk in its pure state from the metal milking-bowls, or made into a delicious rich yoghurt that can be seen regularly at meals all through the region. As the men (never the women) of the Arab desert tribes are responsible for milking their camels, so it is the duty of the Marsh Arab men to milk the family's water-buffaloes. The men also look after the sick buffaloes. They light the small fires that somehow never flame but only smoulder, from which thick spirals of smoke billow round the flanks and eyes of the buffaloes tormented by clouds of summer insects.

The Marsh houses were built then, as they are now, on small islands; one house to an island. Few, if any, of these islands were natural, although after years of human habitation they look very natural indeed. You make one just as Marduk made the world. You decide how big you want your house to be. You gather a small mountain of rushes and heap them in the water inside a reed fence that rises above the surface. When the well-trampled mass of green also appears above the surface, you fold the fencing in on top of it; and continue piling and stamping reeds until you are satisfied with the size and com- pactness of the new island you have just created. To build a more lasting island, you can alternate the layers of reeds and rushes with layers of mud; this solidifies the whole mass of earth and vegetation into a virtually indestructible mound. Abandoned mounds, of varying size, are to be found scattered here and there through the Marshes. People have been building them, in the way I have just described, for five or six thousand years.

At flood-time, you see Marsh householders raising the level of their island floor with fresh rushes. You see them at other times weaving low barriers, perhaps 6 inches high round the buffalo-platforms that project from the rear of houses, 'like,' Gavin Maxwell wrote, 'round after-decks of medieval galleons'. These are not so much to prevent the buffaloes and cows that share the family's living space from escaping – buffaloes are far too lazy and spoiled to want to escape, and cows don't like deep water – as to provide a useful rail to which one can tie up one's canoe.

Presently, unsettled Semitic peoples – Akkadians, Aramaeans – came from the north and the deserts. The mixture of these Semites with the non-Semitic Sumerians produced what we

know as 'Babylonians'. But the buffalo- and fisher-people of the Marshes were not always left in peace. Centuries followed of shift and counter-shift in the power-play of the various states of Mesopotamia – of tooth and claw struggles between their rulers. Then the 'Romans' of the ancient East arrived: the ruthless Assyrians with their irresistible war-machine.

Their blood-and-thunder dominion in the area disrupted a relatively peaceful period between about 1400 and 1000 BC in which the kings of the great powers, Egypt, Babylon, Assyria and the Hittite kingdom in the north, found it best to preserve a careful balance of power. In Babylon, the great King Hammurabi codified laws, built temples, reformed agriculture. But trouble was near. What had been described as the 'barbarous and unspeakable cruelty of the Assyrians' soon overwhelmed the area.

Ashurnasirpal, Shalmaneser, Adadnirari, Tiglathpileser, Sennacherib, Ashurbanipal: the names of the Assyrian kings ring out like the reverberations of barbaric gongs. Sennacherib was the king who, more than any other, impinged on the Marsh Arabs. In his capital Nineveh, from 705 BC he proclaimed himself 'the great king, the mighty king, king of the universe, king of Assyria, king of the four quarters (of the world). . . .'

Soon, two of his lightning campaigns – his war-making ranged across the Middle and Near East from Egypt to southern Persia – shattered the peace of the Marshes. In his first campaign of 703 BC, 'raging like a lion and storming like a tempest' (his own words), he captured Babylon and his charioteers careered south in hot pursuit after the king, Merodachbaladan. The escaping king was lucky enough to reach the Marshes. There, he plunged into the reed-beds, and because the Madan rallied to his assistance, he was safely hidden. However disgruntled he may have felt, Sennacherib caused it to be recorded in his annals, 'I hurried after him (the king) and sent my warriors into the midst of the swamps and marshes and they searched for him for five days, but his hiding place was not found.'

Sennacherib did not, however, return to Nineveh empty-handed. He took 208,000 prisoners and mules, horses, cattle and sheep. 'The people of Chaldea, the Aramaeans . . . who had not submitted to my yoke, I snatched away from their lands, made them carry baskets and mould bricks. I cut down the reed marshes which are in Chaldea, and had the men of the foe whom my hands had conquered drag their mighty reeds (to Assyria).'

A later campaign, in 694 BC, took Sennacherib, still 'raging like a lion', to Elam or southern Persia on the Gulf (the 'Bitter Sea'). To prepare for that expedition, he built ships on the Tigris at Nineveh. When they were ready his cohorts moved down in them to Bab-salimet, at the mouth of the Euphrates.

'My brave warriors (Sennacherib recorded) who know no rest, I embarked in the ships, and provided supplies for the journey and straw for the horses, which I embarked with them. My warriors went down the Euphrates on the ships while I kept to the dry land at their side. . . .' A Marsh flood pinned him and his men in the ships for five days. Then, 'the ships of my warriors reached the swamps at the mouth of the river, where the Euphrates empties its waters into the fearful sea.'

After the Assyrians, came the Chaldeans and Medes who destroyed the Assyrian empire. Then came the neo-Babylonians, whose King Nebuchadnezzar defeated an intruding Egyptian Army in 605 BC. But by 539 BC Babylon was nearly finished. Cyrus the Great of Persia captured it. And after Cyrus came the Greeks. Alexander the Great passed through southeast Mesopotamia on his return from India to Ctesiphon. He died on the Tigris there, possibly from a fever picked up in the swamps. His admiral, Nearchos, established a port near Basra (which did not yet exist) not far from modern Khorramshahr. It was variously known as Alexandria, Antioch and Spasinou Charax. Much merchandise passed through it from India to Arabia. But no trace of it remains today.

The single, most dramatic event in the history of the Near and Middle East, leave alone in the Marshes, was the coming of Islam. By that time, successive migrations of tribes from the Arabian desert ensured that, whether they were by religion Byzantine Christian or heathen, the peoples of southern Iraq were part of the Arab race.

In AD 634, two years after the death of the Prophet Mohammed at Medinah, the dashing Muslim general Khalid bin Walid, appropriately nicknamed 'the Sword of Islam', appeared on the edge of the Euphrates delta with a force of 18,000 Arabian tribesmen. He was the Napoleon of the age. He stormed up to the oases of Iraq fresh from brilliant campaigns in north and central Arabia. So far Khalid's newly Islamized warriors had seen little but desert and mountain. Now these lean, ascetic Arabs of the wilderness stared wide-eyed at what to them was a kind of Paradise. They had never set eyes on canals and greenness like this before, or waving corn, or such *water*. They were, after all, about to descend into a new cradle of civilization and the arts. For that is what this, by now Persian, province, governed by *dihqans*, or Persian district officers, had become. The new civilization had overlaid the older glories. Ur, Babylon, Nimrud and Nineveh of the Assyrians were by now nothing but shapeless mounds. And now even this new and apparently unshakeable power – the Sassanid empire of Persia – was to be swiftly robbed of its fairest acquisition.

First, the wild-eyed fighters of Arabia dispersed a Persian army glittering with princes and nobles at the wells of Hafir on the desert's edge. The Persian soldiers were said to have been bound together to prevent flight and so the battle became known as 'The Battle of the Chains'. The warriors of Khalid bin Walid were soon racing their horses to the Euphrates and hell-for-leather across it through the edge of the reed-beds. The ultimatum Khalid gave out to the people of the region said, in effect: 'Accept the faith and you are safe; otherwise pay tribute. If you refuse to do either, you have only yourself to blame. A people is already upon you, loving death as you love life.'

Khalid's ultimatum worked. The Marsh peoples and peasants were not molested; their lands remained theirs. The Christian tribes of the area agreed to pay tribute and were permitted to remain Christian without further interference. Next, however, the Muslim army suffered a set-back. In November AD 634, the Persian hero, Rustam, the brave and energetic administrator of a corrupt and crumbling empire, rallied his forces. He advanced across the Gharraf with elephants, 'their *howdas* manned with warriors, like moving castles'. He unfurled the imperial banner of panther skins. And he defeated – almost annihilated – the Arabian army near Hirah, west of the Euphrates.

All the same, the Persians were doomed. The Muslims rallied and defeated them at the battle of Boweib in AD 635. And soon, Rustam was killed at Qadisiyah and his Sassanid army routed for good. The Caliph Omar now decreed the founding of two new cities in the south: Basra and Kufa. Both were military bases. The houses in both cities were at first made of reeds; and in both the first mosques were built of reeds and clay, and then clay brick. Both places soon grew into major centres of the Islamic world. Omar named Kufa the capital of newly-conquered Iraq. Basra became the bustling half-way port of commerce between the eastern and western worlds.

The local population welcomed the Arabian soldiers. The tribes of Mesopotamia were mostly Christian at that time and had not been well treated by the Persian Zoroastrians. They felt the Persians to be aliens. Now their ties with the Arabs of the desert, already strong, were reinforced. In the wake of victory, many more desert tribes moved eagerly into the lush Mesopotamian plains. In the markets, and in the fields bordering the waterways and lagoons, these pure Arab camel-breeders from the Peninsula met the Marshmen, learned their ways, married into them, and gave back their new faith, Islam, in return.

Under Ali, the fourth Caliph, Kufa, Basra and the regions surrounding them again became the scene of conflict. Ali had moved his capital to Kufa from Medinah, after assuming the Caliphate. He was the Prophet Mohammed's first cousin, and his son-in-law. But there were many who refused to recognize his accession, and these included the Prophet's favourite and hot-tempered wife, Ayesha, and Zubair bin Awwam and Talha bin Abdullah, two of Mohammed's companions. The three of them raised a tribal army in Basra and despite efforts by Ali, who was an affable man, to avoid a conflict, he was forced into battle. 'The Battle of the Camel' was joined between Ali's tribal forces and those of his opponents in December AD 656. The formidable Ayesha became a rallying-point as she sat prominently in a camel-borne litter (hence the name of the battle) which was soon full of arrows like a pin-cushion. It was a tragic affair. The fighting was fierce and fratricidal: the Beni Rabia of Kufa fought the Beni Rabia of Basra, and other tribes were similarly riven. The noise of the armies coming together was 'like that of washermen at the riverside'. By evening Talha and Zubair were dead. Ali brought down Ayesha, shrilly protesting, from her disabled camel and gently packed her off home to Medinah. Ali was magnanimous. He stayed a few days in Basra and had a large trench dug for the many dead. A small town named after Zubair exists to this day among acacia groves just outside Basra. After this first bloody fight between Muslims, the Marsh people must have returned to their lagoons more thoughtful men.

Ali's conflict with his Syrian-based Umayyad rivals for the Caliphate (which has been compared to the rift between Protestants and Catholics) continued until AD 661. Then this gentle and valiant man was assassinated on his way to the mosque at Kufa. He was buried at Nejef nearby and became a saint to the Shia Muslims.

Ali represents to Muslims, and indeed to all Arabs, the sum of chivalry and virtue; he is the paragon about whom tomes of poems, proverbs and stories have been written. So, to only a slightly lesser extent, is his martyr son Hussein, who marched to Kufa with a pathetic band of 200 supporters to claim his dead father's Caliphate from the Umayyad governor of Iraq, was surrounded at Kerbela by a much larger force and defeated and killed on the tenth day of Muharram AH 61 (10th October, AD 680). Abbas, another of Ali's sons, lost both arms and then his life as he tried to fetch water for his brother Hussein's doomed companions. To a Marsh Arab today, an oath in Abbas' name is the most binding of all oaths. '*B'il Abbas*, by Abbas. . . .' you hear a man cry in a crowded reed *mudhif*, and you see the others nodding, as much as to say, 'Oh well, that's true enough, then'. The Arab rosary (the *Sibha*) is still used, either as 'worry beads' or to obtain Divine Guidance in this fashion: isolate a section of the beads and name them left to right 'Allah, Mohammed, Ali, Hussein, Abu Jahl'. If the final bead coincides with one of the first four names all is well – go ahead with your plan: if the final bead falls to Abu Jahl, a contemporary of the Prophet but an enemy of Islam, call it off. Thesiger and I taught them another system and soon the Marsh echoed to young voices chanting

'Eeny, Meeny, Miney, Mo! Catch a nigger by his toe.
If he squeals let him go. O-U-T spells out so out you must go!'

All Marsh Arabs are nominal Shias, although some pray irregularly and some younger men nowadays do not pray at all. The
shrine cities of Kerbela, where Hussein is buried, and Nejef, are
intensely revered places of pilgrimage and those who make it
are called *Zairs*. You can see *mahailas* (big sailing-barges) on
the Euphrates bearing the coffins of the faithful, Marsh Arabs
among them, to those sacred resting-places.

These exciting and historically crucial events had proved almost
fatal to the agricultural economy on which Iraq depends. The
story of Mesopotamia is, after all, a story of irrigation. The
early Sumerians' skill in reclaiming land has been the wonder
of irrigation experts ever since. Their dykes enclosed vast areas
in which five towns and prosperous villages were settled below
sea-level. The enclosed, reclaimed land was irrigated by means
of openings in the dykes. But later these skilful works were
undone. In the fifth century AD there was one of many periods
of political confusion and administrative neglect. Towns and
fields were flooded as ill-kept dykes crumbled away. Later
mismanagement frustrated further attempts at reclamation. The
destruction of one of the most sophisticated and skilful water-
control systems ever conceived by man was carried yet another
stage farther by the failure in the seventh century AD of a
well-meaning Sassanian king. He mobilized every able-bodied
man in a desperate rescue operation. He even publicly executed
– by crucifixion – forty dyke-builders who had somehow failed
to block a vital breach. All to no avail.

In this dismal decline, the golden age of the Abbasid Caliph,
Harun al Rashid (AD 786–809) in Baghdad represented a mere
breathing space. This magnificent Arab ruler, a more glorious
contemporary of Charlemagne, supervised an energetic pro-
gramme to restore the dykes and canals of the lower Tigris and
Euphrates. Eleven hundred years later, Sir William Willcocks

was to agree with Harun, that by far the best way of re-irrigating
those areas was by re-digging and re-opening the watercourses
of the Babylonians. This, rather than embark on a whole new
scheme, Harun's governors proceeded to try to do. The result
was successful and a further period of agricultural richness.
Barley, wheat, rice, dates, sesame and sugar burgeoned across
the land. It did not last. After Harun and his son, it was
essentially downhill all the way. By AD 1000 the mightiness and
magnificence of Harun's empire had shrunk to a mere province,
weakly and corruptly governed. In 1258 the Caliphate of Baghdad was extinguished for ever by the invasion of Hulagu, the
grandson of Jenghis Khan, and his hordes of Mongol soldiers
on shaggy ponies, who laid waste the 'incomparable sacred
city'. Hulagu made a macabre pyramid of the skulls of Baghdad's poets, scholars and divines and turned Iraq into a governorate of the Mongol rulers in Iran. The superb irrigation
system – the perfect network of dykes with which Harun had
reclaimed tracts of the Marshes – was deliberately destroyed
by Hulagu and finished off, in 1401, by the armies of Timur
the Lame. The garden province, the richest in the Abbasid
empire, degenerated into a water-strangled region of tribal
grazing with a dwindling population in a few towns. Paradise
was lost and has yet to be regained. From then on, the Tigris
slopped its waters unchecked sideways, east and west, below
Kut and on each side of Amara (or where Amara would be
later). The Euphrates overspilled south towards the sea from
Suq-esh-Shiukh. And these flood-waters created new Marshes,
permanent and accepted.

Meantime the population of the Marshes was, of course,
swollen by an influx of Arab refugees fleeing from the Mongol
massacres. And no doubt, the Madan had been joined earlier
by some at least of the survivors of a great slave uprising in the
Basra region against a ninth century Caliph of Baghdad. Its
leader, called Ali the Abominable, made his headquarters in the
Marshes and from the shelter of the reed-beds carried on a
guerrilla war of ambushes and night-raids, actually capturing
Basra before his own capture and execution fourteen years

later. The Caliph's general sent his head to Baghdad, and his rebel army was scattered utterly. How many fugitives found permanent sanctuary in the Marshes? Some, surely.

After the stunning blow of the Mongol invasion the history of Iraq shades into the struggle between Persia and Turkey. The details of it do not closely concern the Marsh Arabs. In the period of Persian hegemony, we know that the Arab governor of Basra paid annual tribute to the Shah. And that when Baghdad fell to the Turkish Sultan, Sulaiman the Magnificent, in 1533, the tribes of the Gharraf, the central and Hawaiza Marshes, and of Basra quickly made obeisance to him. This did not mean that from then on the tribes knuckled down obsequiously to the Turkish Pashas in Baghdad. On the contrary, they remained extremely restless, as is their nature. For example, a large Turkish expedition (300 ships) had to be sent to Basra in 1546. After the battle near Chubaish, the tribes were chased back to their reeds. Yet in 1549, they were in arms again. This time, Ali Pasha Tamarrud, the captain of the Janissaries, the Sultan's finest soldiers, trounced them at Medinah on the Euphrates. But the uncrushable Madan continued to menace the approaches to Basra.

By 1500, Arab traditions were universal in Iraq. From Mosul to Basra, the Arabic language and Arab culture rooted in Islam prevailed. In the south, apart from Basra, the principal townships were Dair (on the Shatt al Arab), Nahr al Antar, Mansuriya, and Kut al Muammir. The modern towns of Amara, Kut al Amara and Nasiriya did not exist before the nineteenth century. The Sultan decreed Basra a *wilaya* (governorate) under the Pasha of Baghdad. And the Wali of Hawaiza ruled the Arab tribes of Arabistan – notably the Kaab – who grew rice and bred buffaloes in the marshes and bush-land that spread across what is now the Iraq-Iran frontier, east of Qurna and the Shatt al Arab towards Ahwaz.

Turbulent times, to say the least, persisted for the next 300 years and more. Basra remained a hornet's nest of trouble for Iraq's Ottoman rulers, despite expedition after punitive expedition sent from Baghdad. Nothing the Pashas did could eradicate those human Arab hornets – crack battalions of Janissaries armed with matchlock firearms, the chopping off of heads, fines, imprisonment – no armies, no punishments had any lasting effect. In the seventeenth century, indeed, Arab hostility became so intense that one Turkish Pasha in Basra could stand no more of it and decamped, handing over his administration (for a sum of money) to an Arab leader called Afrasiyab. Not much is known of Afrasiyab, but his remarkable son, Ali Pasha, in 1624 repulsed a Persian invasion at Qurna with Portuguese naval help, and was altogether a fine cultured specimen of tribal nobility. Ali Pasha's court at Basra was compared by some people to that of Harun al Rashid himself. The arts flourished; government became liberal and humane in this state within the Turkish state. Even the Marsh Arabs were mollified for a time. But only for a time. Ali's graceless offspring, Hussein Pasha, predictably lost the tolerance of the Madan by instituting a buffalo tax. And so, when the Sultan's army finally cornered him at Qurna, he found his tribal allies melting away into the reeds.

By now the united tribes of southern Iraq were a force to be reckoned with. Powerful tribal confederations had been formed. In the mid and lower Tigris area, for example, the great Beni Lam confederation of hair-tented tribes came into being when Hafadh – a great-grandson of a certain Lam – split, due to some dispute, with his overlord of the Hawaiza districts. The Albu Mohammed groupings, south-east and south-west of present-day Amara, which later were to be in conflict with the Beni Lam for decades, also originated in the seventeenth century. Of the Beni Lam, the famous eighteenth century Arabian traveller, Carsten Niebuhr, wrote: 'A great tribe . . . they receive duties upon goods carried between Basra and Baghdad. These Arabs sometimes pillage caravans. The Pasha of Baghdad then sends troops against them, and sometimes chastises them by beheading their chiefs. But the successors of these *Schiechs* (Sheikhs), who have been beheaded, are always as great enemies to the Turks, and as zealous to maintain their liberty, as their predecessors have been.'

The most powerful confederation of all was founded on the lower Euphrates. After a long period of feud and bloodshed, the principal tribes – the Beni Malik, the Ajwad and the Beni Said – in the area between Samawa and the Hor al Hammar – were united under the family of Al Shabib. The whole grouping was famous by 1770, even outside Iraq, as the Muntafiq. Niebuhr mentions that their paramount sheikh was residing at Nahr al Antar near Qurna, and says that they dominated a large number of subaltern tribes, including 'people of the buffalo'. He observed that 'the lands between the Tigris and the Euphrates are intersected by numerous canals and are inhabited only by tribes practising agriculture, or *Moaedan*'.

Of the ordinary people, Niebuhr says: 'They are poor, as must naturally be the condition of the subjects of those sheikhs who live comfortably themselves, but are not disposed to suffer their peasantry to grow rich.' (The man who wrote this was no liberal before his time, but the son of a yeoman of Denmark.) Yet even if they were poor, they could fight. In 1775, three years after Niebuhr's book was published, a full-scale Persian attack on Basra was resisted by an interesting gallimaufry of defenders – Turks, Armenians and Carmelite monks fought shoulder-to-shoulder with Janissaries, Negroes and, last but certainly not least in martial importance, Marsh Arabs. Sheikh Thamir al Sadun of the Muntafiq had brought his men in force into beleaguered Basra. His brother, Abdullah, occupied Zubair. Both towns fell at last. But three years later, the Muntafiq inflicted a devastating defeat on an invading Persian force of 12,000 infantry and cavalry. The Muntafiq sheikh, Thamir, lured the Persians into a trap near Samawa, and, when they were bogged down in the Marshes, charged in with his tribesmen and slaughtered them by the hundred. It was said that only three Persian survivors reached Basra and that the bones of the fallen marked the battle site for a generation.

To this Niebuhr adds: 'The tribe derive their name from one Montefik who came from Hejaz and was descended from a family who were illustrious before the days of Mahomet. One thing certain is that descendants of this Montefik have been foreigners (residents) in this country from time immemorial.' (There is, however, considerable uncertainty – despite the admirable Nieburh's point-blank assertions – about the meaning and origins of the word Muntafiq, which in local dialect is often pronounced Muntafids. Some hold that 'Muntafiq' derives from the Arabic word *Ittifaq* (agreement).)

Niebuhr also comments on two tribes situated eastwards from the Euphrates. The sheikh of one was named Fontil, the other Hamoud. 'They can muster 2000 cavalry, and a proportionate number of infantry. The Pasha of Baghdad has recently made war on these people, with various success. . . . Those tribes which are of a pure Arab race live on the flesh of their buffaloes, cows and horses and on the produce of some little ploughing. . . . These are denominated *Moaedan.*'

In the light of our knowledge of the political evolution of Iraq, it is interesting now to read what Niebuhr wrote in 1770 – that: 'The frequent wars between several tribes and the Pasha of Baghdad, although viewed as rebellion by the Ottoman officers, are proof of the independence of the Arabs.'

The obscure children of the reeds had grown up. What were they originally but peaceful spear-fishers of Sumer, then sanctuary-givers to refugees from Assyrian 'kings of the Universe' and from the Mongolian horsemen of the Steppes? Later the intrusive Shahs and Khans of Persia found a different sort of population. Centuries of unwelcome arrivals – foreign soldiers, tax-gatherers, cattle-rustlers, the predatory henchmen of tyrannical overlords – had bequeathed them an intense suspicion of visitors. They had become, as I found later, brilliant dissimulators. I have observed them talking to officials with an exquisite politeness, as dead-pan and watchful as poker-players.

But another change had occurred. Transformed by constant infusions of the fiery blood of Arabian tribes from Khalid bin Walid and the Caliph Ali's time onwards, the Madan still fished, kept buffaloes and grew rice but they had become fighters, too. Pashas learned to think twice before sending expensive armies to put them in their place. The Marsh people had become Marsh *Arabs* with the shrewd will-o'-the-wisp spirit of their desert kinsmen. *Seba* – lion – they call a brave man; but they say cunning people are *mithel firan* – like mice, cautiously, silently, living on their wits under the ground. And so, the *beau ideal* of the Madan is half-mouse, half-lion: an odd creature but, in its special habitat, not an easy one to snare.

4 The First Europeans

The Marsh Arabs were virtually unknown even in the early 1950s, yet for centuries outsiders, including Europeans, had passed by, and occasionally through, the great reed-beds. Naturally they caught tantalizing glimpses of the Marsh people and were fascinated by them. But they were moving on foot or horse to some distant destination that might take months to reach, and had no time to hang about. Anyway, it was thought inadvisable to loiter among such strange people in such a remote place. Even so, several travellers took the trouble to note down their impressions of the region of Basra and the Marshes. The earliest of these 'modern' travel notebooks dates back to the seventeenth century, and that is my excuse for skipping at this point back to a man who wrote about Mesopotamia some 200 years before Niebuhr. Like most travellers, this man spent some time in and about the city of Basra – the city and its surrounding area closely complement each other – so I include his observations on Basra as well. He is to be found, pestered by mosquitoes and face to face with his first Marsh Arabs.

'Being suspicious of some Arabian Maedi's, that is, Vagrants or Vagabonds (so call'd because they abide with Droves of Buffles) . . . for more security we removed a mile further.' So, in 1625, wrote the bold but cautious Italian nobleman, Pietro della Valle, and in doing so broadcast to the European world, probably for the first time, the word Maedi (or as one would write it today, Madi), the adjective deriving from Madan. Della Valle, who had travelled even further east, was now on his precarious way from Basra to Aleppo. He had spent the previous night under the stars on the edge of the marshes: a most unsatisfactory night, he noted in his diary the next morning. 'We lodged in a place where the multitude of Gnats suffered us to sleep but little.' Earlier he had remarked on the 'many dry lakes and land with abundance of canes . . . and certain reeds and verdant fields.' He had also complained of the bitterness of the water thereabouts.

Still, there were compensating sights of interest. 'The Chaldean Lake is on our right hand,' he observed. 'I saw upon the ground an abundance of Sea-shells, shining within, like Mother-of-Pearl, some whole, and some broken; I wonder'd how they came so far from the Sea. I saw also many pieces of Bitumen, scatter'd up and down, which is produc'd in that brackish soil by the overflowing of the water at some time of the year: I have a piece of it by me to shew.' He also picked up some seals and pieces of black marble with cuneiform writing on them.

In a new spate of travel-writing, seventeenth-century men like della Valle opened doors long closed on the Near East. The glorious Renaissance in Europe, the discovery of the Americas, had thrust places like Mesopotamia out of Western minds. If people in Paris, London, Rome or Madrid considered 'The East' at all, their thoughts flew to the Indies which the thrilling sea-voyages of Vasco da Gama and Diaz had disclosed. Now land-travel was becoming fashionable; it was sometimes more arduous and more interesting than sea-travel. Accounts of journeys almost incredible in their daring were being published by officers, merchants, archaeologists and simple adventurers who preferred, or were obliged by circumstance, to take the overland route home from the Far East. It was a long, tricky haul. Travelling west from India you were almost bound, unless you made a long mountainous detour through Kurdistan, to pass through Basra and up the course of the Euphrates or the Tigris across Syria to the Mediterranean. You took Arab guides, guards and porters from Basra and lots of money. You joined a camel caravan (for safety in numbers) and all being well you reached Aleppo in seventy days.

It was sensible to stay awhile in Basra. Arab guides and perhaps guards had to be recruited from there and it was worth taking time to check their credentials: guides had been known to send news of your impending arrival to marauding tribesmen they were in touch with, who would arrange to ambush you in the desert. It was really best to wait until a caravan had assembled and go with that. Pietro della Valle found Basra (or Bassora as he called it) large and prosperous, but ill-built. 'The people are Arabians with some Turks intermix'd.' There were also some Sabaeans – he erroneously labelled them 'Christians of St John' – who 'speak a harsh Chaldee, besides Arabick which is in general use, which language they also call Mandai (or Mandean).' He admired the verdure of date-trees and cultivated fields and the grand houses and handsome gardens on the canals. On the Shatt al Arab he saw 'Portugal ships' at anchor which had come to lend the Pasha of Basra a hand in warding off an invading Persian Army, led by the Khan of Shiraz; at that very moment the Persians were advancing from the Marsh region of Hawaiza to capture Qurna. In return for a generous payment the Portuguese naval commander, Gonsalvo de Silveiro, had dispatched three ships-of-war to Qurna to shell the Persians. Partly because of them, perhaps, and with news of dissension at home, the Khan called off his campaign in the nick of time. The Pasha marched his men, banners streaming and trumpets proudly snarling, back to Basra in triumph.

Basra had been, in *One Thousand and One Nights*, the city of Sinbad the Sailor: 'a towne of great trade of spices and drugges', Ralph Fitch noted in 1583. During a series of visits from 1638 on, a French nobleman, J. B. Tavernier, described things more exactly: 'The Prince of Balsara [up to the twentieth century the spelling varied wildly] is so good a Husband, that he lays up three millions of livres in the year. His chief revenue is in four things, Money, Horses, Camels, and Date-trees; but in the last consists his chiefest wealth.' Basra had long been a small but glittering emporium on the East-West trade route. 'So much liberty and good order in the city,' wrote Tavernier, 'that you may walk all night long in the streets without molestation. The Hollanders bring spices every year. The English carry pepper and some few cloves; but the Portugals have no trade at all thither. The Indians bring Calicuts, indigo, and all sorts of merchandise. In short there are merchants of all countries from Constantinople, Smyrna, Aleppo, Damascus, Cairo and other parts of Turkie, to buy such merchandise as come from the Indies, with which they lade the young camels which they buy in the place: for thither the Arabians bring them to put them to sale. They that come from . . . Moussel, Baghdad, Mesopotamia, and Assyria send their merchandise up the Tigris by water, but with great trouble and expense.' Implicit in that passage is the fact that the Dutch and British (of the East India Company) had by this time virtually replaced the Portuguese as dominant foreigners in the Gulf, which they had had the run of for a century and where they were universally hated for their cruelty and rapacity. The 'great trouble and expense' refers to the 'Jack-in-the-Box habits of the tribes of the lower Tigris and Euphrates – the Muntafiq and the Beni Lam and Albu Mohammed, as well as the remoter Madan tribes.

These tribesmen, exotically bearded and ringletted, were forever bobbing up and demanding a hefty toll as the price of further passage through their territories. Sometimes tribesmen accosted passers-by firmly but courteously; at other times they displayed a surly impatience. It depended on their mood. In their blackest mood a traveller might be stripped to his underwear. At any rate, almost anyone might get the shock of a lifetime when a posse of apparently ferocious and hostile tribesmen, brandishing spears and swords, came charging down out of the desert or the reeds. So, as I have said, it was worth spending a few days preparing for the trip in Basra – assuming all was well there.

For things were not always well in Basra. The city was the victim of flood, plague and invasion at regular intervals until the twentieth century. Invading Persian armies stormed out of Shiraz, seized the great port and expelled Turkish Pashas; successive Pashas of Baghdad sent down Janissary armies which chased the Persians back across Arabistan. A great deal of blood was shed by all concerned. Whoever held the city, from its depths arose awesome smells from hopelessly inadequate sanitation. Pestilence lurked in its bazaars. Yet its peculiar beauty rose above these drawbacks: visitors sang Basra's praises in book after book. By 1797, 'Bussora (yet another variation in spelling) was very large and extremely populous', according to John Jackson, Esq., who stepped off there on his way from India to London. He jotted down: 'Bazaar nearly two miles long . . . European manufactures scarce and dear (people prefer those of England to all others) . . . a Roman Catholic Church – the people of that persuasion are not in the least molested.' His eulogy continued: 'A party of us went a-shooting. . . . Beside the date (we found) there were great quantities of pomegranets nearly all ripe; and abundance of oranges, limes and lemons which gave out a fragrant smell. . . . I was very much pleased with this little journey; and though I had lately been in the island of Ceylon among the cinnamons . . . I certainly should give the preference to this place. A most delightful spot. The inhabitants, too, were remarkably civil.' Arriving in 1817, after one of the many Basra plagues, Lieutenant William Heude of the Madras Military Establishment, expected trouble there – he had been warned that foreigners were unwelcome. To his relief, as he wrote home later, 'we never met with the slightest annoyance or incivility'. He stayed with the British Resident, Dr Colquhoun, who kept forty to fifty Arab horses, and as he departed for Baghdad, 'our bark glided smoothly down the stream, passing the little date gardens on its bank, where many a wealthy lascivious Turk sat reclining in the full enjoyment of coffee, slothfulness and his *chubook* (water-pipe)'. The coffeehouses, too, were full of lounging Janissaries, puffing pipes.

Skipping a period of about a hundred years, another Briton, this time a naval artist, expressed scepticism about the claims of Basra to the title 'Venice of the East' because of its canals. And surely not *every* house, he complained, could be the former abode of Sinbad the Sailor, as everybody claimed. But even he succumbed to the spirit of the place – 'Basra can boast no architecture, but Nature can surpass in beauty anything that Venice can show. The artificially dug channels among the gardens are beautiful beyond description; the date glades reflect in the still water, dream-like and enchanting.' He saw, particularly at twilight, mystery and romance in the old houses, the water, the gondola-like boats; and he reflected it all in his remarkable sketches.

For those early travellers, the tentative way north followed two routes. One wavered over the dusty plain to the small town of Zubair (where Ali the Barmecide of *One Thousand and One Nights* is buried) and from there north across the desert to the Euphrates: della Valle took this route. The other followed the Shatt al Arab to Qurna and thence up the Tigris to Baghdad or on the westward-running Euphrates to Suq-esh-Shiukh, Samawa, Hilla and Baghdad. At Qurna (also spelled Corny, Koorna and Kurnah by successive diarists) by 1800, a ramshackle Turkish ship-of-war habitually lay in the Tigris to prevent merchant vessels passing without paying customs. Now and again it fired off a gun to give a spurious impression of alertness, but it was not sea-worthy. Every traveller remarked on the lush beauty of Qurna. Colonel Chesney, on a series of British expeditions in 1835, 1836 and 1837 to chart the waters of both the Tigris and Euphrates, remarked on the particular excellence of the dates of this part of the lower Euphrates (Pliny, however, had written that in his day the Tigris, not the Euphrates, was 'the most fertile of the East' – *solum Orientis fertilissimum*). Chesney also commented on the depth and width of the Shatt al Arab at the confluence of the two great rivers. The water ran at five to six knots here. (In 1857 a fleet of the largest British Indiamen, including the *Eastern Monarch* of 2000 tons, managed to reach Qurna with an armed force under General Outram in a campaign against the Persians.)

Colonel Chesney's paddle-steamer *Euphrates*, belching smoke from its towering funnel, covered the seventy-five miles from Qurna to Suq-esh-Shiukh in seven and a half hours steaming against the tide. At Suq he remarked on more than 'some 1500 clay-built houses and as many tents: pleasantly shaded by vines, fig and pomegranet trees, interspersed with rose-bushes'. J. Baillie Fraser, in 1834, saw 'a walled town of considerable size. Devastated by the plague which lately depopulated Baghdad and which did not spare the Montefic. . . .' He wandered through the Bazaar ('rather extensive') and found shops filled with 'articles suitable for Arabs alone; spears, daggers, swords and shields, saddles, abbas (cloaks). There were plenty of grocers and druggists: loaves of white sugar, coffee and coarse spices were abundant, as well as the common articles of brown sugar from India, dates, soap, etc., etc.' Fraser, who was not enjoying his trip at all, added grumpily – 'But I looked in vain for a china cup to replace our broken teacups.' Despite the lack of crockery, Fraser was amazed by the volume of trade passing up the Euphrates from Suq-esh-Shiukh – 'In spite of all dangers and imposts. Much of it goes all the way to Damascus.' Travellers also noted Arabs skimming about like mayflies in small fragile canoes made of reeds coated with bitumen. Called *zaimas*, these tiny boats were the cheap *mash-hufs* of that time.

Fraser soon grasped a basic element of Iraq's history from earliest times to the present: 'The whole bank of the Euphrates, often on both sides from Semava (Samawa) to Bussora (Basra),' he recorded, 'exhibits evidences of former dense population and cultivation. . . . What a country it would be under a wise and steady government!' In 1830, yet one more great flood had swept away most of the dykes and swamped the low land down to Basra. Fraser heard that Sheikh Isad of the Muntafiq was near Qurna with some of his men doing their best to repair one of the major dykes. But chronic damage had been done long before 1831. Local tribes alone could hardly restore a whole irrigation system. Expert organization from Baghdad was needed and, alas, the government of the Turks was neither wise nor steady.

What did the Arabs of the area look like? Captain the Hon. George Keppel, passing up the Tigris in 1824, found himself among people who resembled the ancient heroes of Greece and Rome. 'The Arab boatmen were as hardy and muscular-looking

fellows as ever I saw. One loose brown shirt, of the coarseness
of sack-cloth, was the only covering of the latter. This, when
labour required it, was thrown aside, and discovered forms
most admirably adapted to their laborious avocations; indeed,
any of the boatmen would have made an excellent model for
an Hercules; and one in particular, with uncombed hair and
shaggy beard, struck us all with the resemblance he bore to
statues of that deity.' Later, even J. Baillie Fraser, his stomach
still churning since Sheikh Isad's thoughtless offer of a sheep's
eyeball at a tribal feast, admitted that it was remarkable, 'that
a people living among bogs and fens, should be the stoutest,
fairest, and comeliest of all the Arabs'. In Keppel's day, they
were mainly armed with long spears or massive clubs. They
wore turbans or headcloths, and in the Samawa area these were
predominantly red and yellow with long plaited fringes. In the
Lamlum district, and probably elsewhere, tribesmen greased
their hair and wore it 'in several long tails'.

The Marsh women were amazingly handsome, too. Keppel throws in some descriptive detail. The women, like the men, wore loose shirts (he says), and nose-rings and necklaces of silver coins. Some dressed their hair in long plaits studded with coins. 'They were all more or less tattooed on the face, hands, and feet and some were marked on the ankles with punctures resembling the clock of a stocking.' He goes on: 'several women, accompanied by a host of children, brought milk, butter and eggs for sale, and followed the boat for some time. . . . They came to our boat with the frankness of innocence and there was a freedom in their manners, bordering perhaps on the masculine; nevertheless their fine features and well-turned limbs produced a *tout ensemble* of beauty, not to be surpassed perhaps in the brilliant assemblies of civilized life.' Fraser, irritated by the episode of the sheep's eyeball, was still sufficiently impressed to concede that the Marsh women were 'light coloured and beautiful'. It was a general view. As he approached the Shatt al Arab from Hawaiza in 1840, Henry Austen Layard (later Sir Henry Layard and the future excavator of Nineveh and Nimrud), struggling with the infernal heat and flushing lions from the bushes, came at last to reed huts belonging to families of Hawaiza buffalo keepers who were unable to provide corn or grass for his horses. He saw a large Marsh village with herds of buffalo, camels and sheep and a *mudhif* (guest house) where the hospitable Sheikh provided him with a breakfast of fish, curds and buffalo cream. 'Remarkable specimens of Arab beauty', he thought the unveiled Madan women; and he, too, noted it.

Layard had already committed to paper the fact that the best way of proceeding to Baghdad through the volatile tribal area was up the Tigris in one of the East India Company's two small, armed steamers *Assyria* and *Nitocris*. The only other way, he confirmed, was via the postal service route along the 'dangerous edge of the Marsh tribes and Bedowins up to Samawa' – i.e. north from Zubair. He himself tried both ways. Once, with Lieutenant Selby of the Indian Navy who commanded *Assyria* on the Tigris 'run', he stopped the night at the camp of the great

Sheikh Madhkur, paramount chief of the Beni Lam, who went aboard and inspected the steamer's machinery. The Wali of Hawaiza had warned Layard that the Beni Lam were 'of ill repute, treacherous and cruel' and certainly the area was uneasy: the Beni Lam tribes seemed to be at war almost continuously, often against the Pasha of Baghdad, or in squabbles among themselves. But though Layard had some difficulties with Sheikh Madhkur, it was by marauding scallywags of the Bedouin Shammar tribe near Baghdad that he was later almost completely stripped and robbed, not by Arabs of the Marsh region.

Of course, as always, some people provoked trouble through their own stupidity. Troubles were not inevitable. John Jackson, for example, had none on his wanderings in 1797; he seems to have been a cheery person. Forty years later, however, Colonel Chesney was taken aback by a sudden surge of animosity from the people of Suq-esh-Shiukh against his steam paddle-ships *Euphrates* and the Indian mail *Hugh Lindsay*. The women of the tribes, to his intense anxiety, began to pelt the ships with sticks and mud-balls. It became dangerous to go ashore. Dismayed, the Colonel called for an urgent investigation. The danger, he soon discovered, had been due to 'the injudicious distribution' of some religious tracts brought by a German missionary called Mr Samuel. 'Some of these papers had fallen into the hands of the Sheikh of the Montefik, and he, as well as the people at large, became much incensed at the attempt thus made to convert them to Christianity.' The Colonel, fortunately, was able to satisfy the Sheikh that he too had uncontrollable elements to deal with, and that his expedition had no missionary role whatever. At Lamlum, higher up the Euphrates, there was another, potentially more serious, misunderstanding. Colonel Chesney had just scribbled down that the dwellings of the 'numerous population were prettily constructed reed-houses which are portable'. He had also had time to record, uneasily, a sudden appearance of mosquitos of 'unusual size'. Then in the twinkling of an eye and quite unaccountably the local Beni Hacheim tribesmen turned nasty. Groups of them, armed, seemed to be on the warpath. Worse still – 'Mr Ainsworth was on shore at this time, collecting botanical specimens in the adjoining wood, when we perceived that the Arabs were preparing to seize him.' The prompt firing of a Congreve rocket from the boat restored the situation. Once more the Colonel investigated. And once more, when explanations came, the British Expedition turned out to be at fault. Someone, apparently without asking the Colonel's permission, had hacked down part of a wood belonging to the Beni Hacheim. It had been touch and go; and Mr Ainsworth and his specimens had had a close shave. Even so, things could have been worse, and the dutiful Colonel (later General) Chesney put it down in black and white that these were the only instances of hostility in a long-drawn-out expedition.

Of course, Europeans, though their scarlet, lumpy faces, solar topees and button-boots must surely have appeared odd to the Arabs, were no less strange to Marsh tribesmen than the tribesmen were to Europeans. From their shadowy reed doorways, the Madan had peered, seeing but unseen, at *Frenjis* (Franks, to Europeans) passing by in boats; they had tried to get a closer look at della Valle, but he moved off when he spotted them; they had gawked at Europeans within touching distance in bazaars. Marsh Arabs occasionally visited Basra, Zubair, and Qurna, for shopping or gossip, as well as nearer towns like Suq-esh-Shiukh, Mansuriya, Samawa and Kut al Muammir. (In 1694, after all, the mighty confederation of Muntafiq tribes under Mani bin Mughamis actually occupied the port of Basra.) But Europeans in the streets of Basra would hardly have known that these sturdy, darkish-skinned figures in long dingy cloaks gliding by were Marsh Arabs, even if they had noticed them. So, close inspection of the Madan in their native surroundings must have amazed most travellers and frightened others.

Up to modern times even Iraqi townsmen did not know quite what to make of them. Keppel was advised by the Captain of his Arab guards not to risk a visit to a Marsh Arab village, but he bravely did so and survived. He reported – 'The village was a collection of about fifty mat huts from thirty to sixty feet

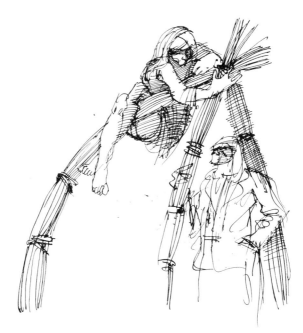

long. The frame of the huts somewhat resembled the ribs of a ship inverted.' Fraser said the east bank of the Euphrates was covered for miles and miles with 'small houses made of split reeds ... which gave the appearance of little gothic-built churches'.

Layard gives a fine pen-picture of a *mudhif* and pays a handsome tribute to its builders. About forty foot long, twenty foot broad and fourteen foot high, it was not by any means the biggest *mudhif* to be seen in the Marshes – there have been some a hundred foot long. But Layard was impressed. Its entrances, he saw, were formed by clusters of long canes fixed in the ground, and united at the top so as to form pointed arches. 'These fluted columns, as it were, were about six feet apart, and between them, serving as a sort of screen, were trellises made of reeds, joined by a twisted worsted or bright colours worked into fanciful designs. Suspended mats, beautifully made and of the finest texture, could be raised or lowered at pleasure so as to admit the air or to exclude the sun. At the side of each column was placed the trunk of a tree shaped into a kind of pedestal, upon which stood a jar of porous clay, such as are used in Arabia for cooling water. These jars, of very elegant form, were constantly replenished from the river, and nothing could be more refreshing than a draught from them. The floor was covered with fine carpets and matting. . . . In order to cool the temperature of the air within the *mudhif* black slaves were constantly throwing water over the mats which were hung up around it and formed the walls. . . . *The remarkable elegance of its construction did infinite credit to the taste and skill of its Arab builders, who were true architects in the best sense of the word.*' (My italics)

Venturing further among the Madan, Fraser found 'some squalor'. Nevertheless, he squatted down among the Marsh Arab families and astonished them by lighting a 'Promethean match' (the fore-runner of the lucifer or phosphorus match) by a stroke of his knife or his pistol butt. They were delighted when he produced a sketch-book and pencil (he was impressed by their fine features) and began to draw them. They could never have seen sketching materials before – 'But they comprehended with surprising quickness somewhat of their use; and when they did so, it was truly amusing to see them first come forward to have their portraits taken and then, like a coquettish child, hiding their faces and running away, or pushing others of their friends into what I suppose they thought a scrape'. The familiar charm of the Marsh people and their love of a game comes vividly through in that short passage written a 150 years ago.

Exact observations illuminate those travellers' notebooks like sodium flares in a cave. Keppel describes how a Marsh Arab tackled a meal – 'After crossing his legs and adjusting his robes with true Arab gravity, he proceeded to business by baring his arm to the elbow; he then grasped a handful of rice, and moulded it into a shape, and I had almost said, the consistence, of a tennis ball. Large as it was, the palatable bolus found its way down his throat, with the aid of a huge lump of butter, with which it was accompanied.' The description holds good today. And so does John Jackson's account from 1797 of Marsh Arab women making bread: 'They have a small place built with clay, between two and three feet high, having a hole at the bottom for the convenience of drawing out the ashes, something similar to a lime kiln. The oven (which I think is the proper name for this place) is usually about 15 inches wide at the top, and gradually grows wider at the bottom. It is heated with wood, and when sufficiently hot, and perfectly clear from smoke, having nothing but clear embers at bottom (which continue to reflect great heat), they prepare the dough in a large bowl, and mould the cakes to the desired size on a board or stone placed near the oven. After they have kneaded the cake to a proper consistence, they pat it a little, then toss it about with great dexterity in one hand, till it is as thin as they choose to make it. They then wet one side of it with water, at the same time wetting the hand and arm with which they put it in the oven. The wet side of the cake adheres fast to the side of the oven till it is sufficiently baked, when, if not paid proper attention to, it would fall down among the embers. If they were not exceedingly quick at this work, the heat of the oven would burn the skin from off their hands and arms; but with such amazing dexterity do they perform it, that one woman will continue keeping three or four cakes at a time in the oven till she has done baking. This mode, let me add, does not require half the fuel that is made use of in Europe.' Jackson's only omission is a further description of how delicious such bread is to eat. But he is such a cheerful traveller that he makes up for that in an unexpected way: he gives a rare and rousing salute to, of all things, the water. 'I cannot quit the Euphrates,' he says, 'without taking notice of its salubrious water, which is by much the most pleasant that I ever tasted. Though muddy when it is first taken up, it soon becomes perfectly clear; and while I could get this water, I had not the least desire for either wine or spirits.' I agree with Mr Jackson. The Marsh Arabs drink it all the time. You see them in their *mashhufs* stretching their hands into the water, inclining their heads downward a fraction, and effortlessly tossing fistfuls of water into their open mouths. But the Euphrates and Tigris water – leave alone the waters of the Marshes – are maligned by Europeans and even by town-bred

Iraqis. 'Wouldn't drink that without boiling it a few times, old man,' Basra Britons used to rumble. I have drunk gallons of it over the years, without noticeable ill effect.

Fraser decided to explore the less frequented Gharraf branch of the Tigris. He ignores in his writings the properties of the water although he, like other sensible travellers in such a hot and humid region, foreswore strong liquor while he was in Iraq. On the other hand, he does enthusiastic justice to the local tea and coffee; it was obviously exactly as it is today: 'Ginger tea was handed round by a black imp of a slave; thickish, syrupy and sometimes flavoured with a little cardomon or cloves.' He was offered the tea in the house of an old sheikh of the Muntafiq. Later he took to Arab coffee – 'as deep in hue as the slave who served it, strong as brandy and as bitter as gall, but fine, warm, refreshing stuff.' During this hospitality, the sheikh plied Fraser with a few basic questions about the outside world: How many kings in Fereng (the land of the Franks)? – Which of them was the most powerful? – Which were stronger, the Russians or the English? And shortly afterwards, the canny old sheikh did his best to palm off a present of a pair of rickety horses on Fraser (a present of some sort was required by the laws of hospitality); Fraser was furious. 'Those nags are not worth ten shillings', he huffed indignantly, and he tried in vain to give them back.

'Mean and ungracious', was Fraser's final description of that particular sheikh. On the other hand, Lieutenant William Heude wrote that 'the pen cannot describe the unassuming courtesy, the open, generous hospitality of these lawless robbers of the desert.' (Despite the 'lawless robbers', he clearly intended that as an unqualified compliment.) One day, near the Gharraf, a member of his group – a slovenly and loudmouthed Turkish 'interpreter' – managed to achieve the unthinkable: in a mind-less burst of Ottoman arrogance, he succeeded in insulting and enraging a gathering of Arab tribesmen in the guest-house of his host, a young Muntafiq sheikh, to a point very close to violence. Heude, the 'infidel', was suddenly in peril. But he and his company were saved by the sheikh, who, though young, knew what tribal honour required. He strode into the melée and quelled the uproar, shouting, 'Friend or foe, believer or infidel, you all enjoy the protection of our tents!'

The densest depths of the Marsh, of course, sheltered large numbers of poor Madan huddling in squalid reed hovels, shaggy, cunning and wild, without government or sheikhs to enforce the traditional discipline. Yet in the great sweep of water and land from Samawa to Hawaiza, where in those days the sheikhs enforced their jurisdiction, Heude, Layard and many other travellers saw that codes of conduct towards visitors were usually in accord with the immemorial tribal lore of the Arabian desert.

5 The Coming of the British

First came the sound of the guns; and such guns. The Marsh Arabs had heard cannons before, but the thunder of these monsters rolling up from the direction of Basra was something quite new – and getting closer. It was 1915, the British were coming, and the end of 400 years of Turkish rule in Iraq was near. The signs of approaching war had been accumulating. For months the Madan – who have an efficient 'reed telegraph' system – had known something was up. For one thing, the Ṭukish authorities had become unusually generous; *chiswas*, or presents of clothes, had been handed out to the sheikhs, and monies long owed had suddenly and most unexpectedly been paid. Barge-loads of Turkish soldiers and war-dancing tribesmen passed purposefully southwards on the Tigris, tossing Marsh Arab *mashhufs* about in their wash. Then from Istanbul the Sultan's proclamation came: *jehad* – a Muslim holy war against the infidel British. The Turks, as Sunni Muslims, hoped to rally the Arab Muslims of Iraq. Presently a British and Indian force under General Barrett landed at Basra.

Basra, its Customs House ablaze, was easily occupied. So were Zubair and Shuaiba, five miles north. At Qurna there was quite a battle. Gata bin Shamkhi, the flag-bearer of Sheikh Falih of the Albu Mohammed, who sent men to fight for the Turks, breathlessly broke the news of it in Qalat Salih, and it spread like a Marsh-fire to the chattering tribesmen who eagerly thronged into the *mudhifs* throughout the region. Qurna, he reported, had fallen to the British troops. One thousand Turkish soldiers had been taken and with them the Turkish Wali of

Basra, Subhi Bey. The Turkish gun-boats, *Marmaris* and *Bulbul*, had been beached and shelled and set on fire five miles north of Al Azair by the Royal Naval gun-boat, *Clio*. Seeing their 'allies' the Turks in disarray, the Arab tribal levies from further north prudently dispersed back to their black tents and flocks; Marsh Arabs dived back into the reeds. The Madan elders who went cautiously to Qurna to see who was in charge there, were well received by Arabic-speaking British officers but had difficulty in pronouncing the name of the newly installed British Political Officer who was called Crosthwaite.

Not every tribal sheikh rushed to greet the British. Far from it. The Turks had handed out medals and cash to important sheikhs and these gifts in some cases paid off, particularly east of the Tigris and north of Suq-esh-Shiukh. General Barrett had quite a tricky time dealing with the Hawaiza Marsh tribes, the Beni Turuf and the Bawi. His Indian cavalrymen were bedevilled equally by Sheikh Falih, son of Sayhud el Munshid and Abd el Karim, son of Zubun al Faisal of the Beni Lam, and by Ghadhban bin Khalaf of the Al Isa. The cavalry were forced to use the narrow pig-tracks through the swamps. Quite a lot of ugly skirmishing took place between the British and the Arabs in that area, and a good many casualties were suffered by each side, particularly as Sheikh Ghadhban paid attractive rewards for any enemy heads brought to him. However, in Sheikh Khazal of the Muhaisin tribe on the Shatt al Arab the British found an ally – luckily, because they had a supply problem and he helped to solve it. *Mashhufs* loaded with dates, fish (which the Punjabi troops would not eat), ducks, chickens, eggs; *bellams* full of sheep, and even some decrepit old water-buffaloes, varied a mournful army diet of bully beef and biscuits.

To the east, the British were opposed mainly by Muntafiq tribesmen and some of the Middle Euphrates. At the battle of Shuaiba 18,000 tribesmen joined the Turkish army and when it was routed by General Nixon's force, the Muntafiq rapidly scurried back to their homes, leaving, it was said, 2000 dead and wounded on the field. Turkish hopes of a major *jehad* campaign with the universal, enthusiastic support of their co-religionists, the tribesmen, fizzled out there and then.

The great Muntafiq confederation was not, in any case, what it once had been – almost a separate Arab nation on the Euphrates. True, the Sadun family was still the nominal overlord of the united tribes. But the Turks had handed out title deeds over vague estates in the Marsh and tribal areas, and the Saduns had become landlords rather than sheikhs. One of them, Nasir Pasha, became *Mutasarrif* (Turkish-appointed governor) of his own district and, in the 1870s, founded the town of Nasiriya. Some of his family objected to this collaboration with the Ottomans, so there were feuds and, bit by bit, the Muntafiq patchwork began to fall apart. But by the time the British came, the confederation was still formidable enough to rack the nerves of their generals.

In fact, the tribes, aiding the Turks, gave General Gorringe, one of the best British commanders, a miserable time when he advanced to take Nasiriya in July, 1915. Gorringe marshalled his force at Qurna in the heat and sweat of high summer then, accompanied by two armed launches, *Odin* and *Espiègle*, moved up the Euphrates to Chubaish. Here, 'Arabs in their graceful *mashufs* . . . scurried to and fro over the lake (the Hor al Hammar), obviously not wishing to do battle with us'. But after Suq-esh-Shiukh the idyll vanished – partly because of the Turkish resistance, partly because of heat and sickness, and partly because of the increasing hostility and resistance of local tribes. At Nasiriya, General Gorringe halted. He was obliged to; the Gharraf tribes resisted his men too fiercely to make a further advance worthwhile.

In any case, the more important town of Amara, which dominated the essential waterway to the north – the Tigris – had already fallen to the British. Amara had been built in 1866 and by 1915 was a town of broad streets and 10,000 inhabitants. It fell to General Townshend with little resistance. The British force seized *mahaila* after *mahaila* (river barge) packed with Turkish troops, as Mohammed Pasha Daghistani's army fell back. Already thrilled by the rush of events the Marsh Arabs

had their first sight of British reconnaisance aeroplanes, two of
which flew up from Basra and low over their heads. It was a
bad time *and* a good time for the Madan. When not running
for cover or taking pot-shots at the planes, they amassed un-
imagined loot. Years later, when I commented on the quantity
of Turkish and British rifles I saw around me in Marsh villages,
an old man said, 'We filled our canoes with stolen rifles then as
we fill them with rushes nowadays. The Turkish war! What a
time that was!'

For the thirty or forty years before the British landings, the
Beni Lam and Albu Mohammed – the two great confederations
lying astride the Tigris north of Al Azair – had been mainly
occupied fighting each other. In 1880, tribal unrest closed the
Tigris for a time, and the regular steamer *Khalifah*, run by the
British company Lynch Brothers, was attacked. As a result, the
Turks built new military cantonments at Amara, the Albu
Mohammed sheikh, Saihud, was given a drubbing by a Turkish
force from Baghdad, and in general Turkish control became
tighter, aided by the newly introduced telegraph and swifter
communication by steamboat.

A major reason why the Tigris tribes gave the British so little
trouble was that the power and wealth of the sheikhs depended
on the ruling power's allotment of leases to their great estates.
As the tide of war flowed northwards the sheikhs of the confederations found themselves at sixes and sevens, not knowing
from month to month if the Turks were beaten for good or
would rally and drive the British into the sea. Thus, Araibi
Pasha al Munshid of the Albu Mohammed and his nephew,
Majid al Khalifah, at first sided with the Turks. But with the
fall of Amara to General Townshend they hastened to pay their
respects to the newly-installed British Political Officer there.
They and other sheikhs were rewarded by reduced rents and
confirmed leases.

In 1916 the Turks forced General Townshend to retreat from
Ctesiphon and captured his entire army at Kut al Amara. British
losses from the fighting, disease, heat and drowning in the
Marshes, mounted horrifyingly, and in London the conduct of

the war was condemned in retrospect as a national disgrace. On the Arab side, the back-and-forth nature of this terrible campaign hopelessly confused the opportunistic sheikhs. How were they to tell who would win? Shabib al Mizban of the Beni Lam, for example, was unalterably pro-British. Others, after vacillating this way and that, misjudged things and ended up pro-Turkish, forced to make the best of the final British victory.

The British setback at Ctesiphon affected tribes elsewhere. General Gorringe, for instance, moving up the Gharraf towards Shatra, was forced to return to Butaniya, near Nasiriya, when he was attacked by 3000 tribesmen who had calculated that the British troops were on the run for good. At Butaniya, tribesmen of the Azairij and Khafaja under Sheikh Khayun al Ubaid engaged the British and Indian soldiers hand-to-hand and killed about 180 of them. No further British advance up the Gharraf was attempted for three years.

On the other hand, at Chubaish, the British simply dismissed the unfriendly paramount sheikh of the Beni Assad, Salim al Khayun, and put his brother Majid in his place.

Very powerful characters like Khayun al Ubaid of the Ubuda tribe in the Shatra area, and Badr al Rumaiyidh of the Albu Salih and paramount sheikh of the Beni Malik, which represented one third of the Muntafiq confederation, shrugged in the face of the inevitable and accepted the British – but only after an expensive and quite futile British effort to capture or kill them.

Badr al Rumaiyidh was a 'tall, heavy, prepossessing figure of a man of sixty-five years, with a rugged face, deep, penetrating eyes'. He was more than just a shifty intriguer. He made an 'unforgettable impression' on Bertram Thomas, the Political Officer at Shatra (who in jocular respect called Badr 'the Old Man of the Marshes'), and on Thomas's boss, Major Harold Dickson, at Nasiriya (the administrative headquarters of the Muntafiq district), and not an easy man to impress. Four hundred infantrymen, 200 levies of the Muntafiq Horse, 100 of the Suq-esh Shiukh scouts, three aeroplanes and two gun-boats were assembled to pursue Badr and his men into the

Marshes, and they were supported by armed tribesmen of the Albu Said, Al Bazun and Al Isa. Even so, Badr escaped. Much later, when Dickson had been replaced by Major A. H. Ditchburn, Badr galloped up to capitulate in his own good time near the Hor al Hammar. 'Approaching Ditchburn (Thomas wrote) he bent down and removed his head-dress. And in the manner of the country tied it slowly to the leg of the chair of those to whom he was making submission.' Relations thereafter were cordial and – most important – based on mutual respect, for there was nothing petty about men like Badr or Ditchburn.

There is a necessary word to be said here about the British Political Officers – an important addition to the Iraqi landscape of the time. These widely scattered and learn-as-you-go young men were remarkable by any standards. They spoke good Arabic; unlike their Turkish predecessors they got about their districts with zest despite heat, insects, water and mud. Surrounded by armed tribesmen, few, if any, of them had British soldiers at hand for their day-to-day protection; at most they were given a section of uncertain Iraqi levies. They may not have been infallible but they were probably not particularly unjust either. They were all deeply interested in the tribes and the landscape. They were often amateur anthropologists, ornithologists or archaeologists. Their success depended largely on their strength of character for, in the tribal chiefs, they confronted men of equal will and greater immediate power.

Thomas, whom I have already mentioned, later became the first non-Arab to cross the great Empty Quarter of Arabia on foot and camel. Dickson became British Political Agent in Kuwait, settled there, and wrote a standard work on *The Arab of the Desert*. H. St John Philby, the second man to cross the Empty Quarter, later became the friend and adviser of King Abdul Aziz ibn Saud, the mighty welder of the Hejaz and Arabia Deserts into Saudi Arabia, mapped much of the kingdom, and wrote numerous books about his travels in the Arabian Peninsula. (He was also the father of Kim, the notorious British diplomat who defected to the Russians.)

At the time of which I am writing Philby was the arabophile, though truculent, Political Officer of Amara. One who soon succeeded him there was S. E. Hedgcock who, with his young wife, wrote a wonderfully vivid book about the people he administered called *Haji Rikkan: Marsh Arab*, using (because officials are not supposed to write books when they are on the job) the pseudonym 'Fulanain'. Other notable civilians were Stephen Longrigg (now Brigadier), the author of two scholarly – and indispensable – works on Iraq; and Captain Gerald Leachman, an experienced Arabian traveller and Arabic speaker, whose name – *Lijman* from Arab mouths – still cropped up in Marsh villages as late as 1952. The 'top brass' of the British administration in Baghdad was unusual: Gertrude Bell, the Oriental Secretary, Sir Percy Cox, the first High Commissioner, and Lt-Colonel (later Sir) Arnold Wilson, were scholars and Arabic speakers, and, in the case of two of them, Miss Bell and Wilson, archaeologists, writers and explorers as well. Whatever the pros and cons of their achievement in Iraq, such people were not second-rate.

The Marsh Arabs left their mark upon the memories of these transient dwellers in Mesopotamia. 'Oh, I was very fond of them!' Mrs Hedgcock exclaimed when I went to see her while preparing this book. 'We both were, my husband and I,' she said – and she brought out with reverence photographs she had taken in 1921 of the familiar *mashhufs* and reed houses along the Chahala. Her late husband's affection for the Madan speaks for itself in their joint book *Haji Rikkan*, which is based on his experience with the eastern Marsh tribes. 'Here dirt and disease should have given death an easy victory,' he wrote. 'Yet here was life triumphant.'

Philby, on a trip to inspect the new railway line from Basra that had just reached Khamisiya, took a lift across the Hor al Hammar in 'a vessel with a penthouse structure of reeds like a Noah's Ark'. He found it was 'pleasant and comfortable, travelling in the always gay company of the Marsh Arabs'. Delayed by a furious storm, he had to spend a night on a large flat island in the lake. There, the Marsh Arabs who lived on it made him welcome and killed a lamb and made 'one of the most delicious meals I ever tasted'. Elsewhere, echoing his compatriots a hundred years earlier, Thomas commented ecstatically on the 'laughing moon faces (of the Marsh girls) their hair plaited with coloured beads, their large flashing eyes and dazzling teeth'. Hedgcock noted that the men still wore their hair thick and long in two plaits and a single coarse-woven shirt. And when a friend took Philby up in a DH9 aeroplane he saw areas of water that 'were more like inland seas than lakes'.

Philby and the rest of them were open-air, down-to-earth men: they preferred to be out and about with Arabs than deskbound in Basra (where Philby spent some time as Revenue Commissioner). Philby had horrified Lady Cox there by dipping a cup into the Shatt al Arab and drinking from it, and he scoffed at Army Orders that forbade eating dates from the trees on health grounds. The genteel tennis, hockey and river picnics organized by the wives of the garrison at Amara bored him. He was much more interested in meeting Araibi Pasha of the Albu Mohammed – 'a very old man, though still full of fire'. Proceeding further down the Chahala by launch, he found Gerald Leachman – 'an erratic genius', according to Philby – trying to buy sheep for the British forces from Sheikh Ghadhban of the Beni Lam. Leachman was not an easy man, but nor was Ghadhban who had driven his sheep into the hills of Persia and out of reach. Leachman and Philby had different ideas about how to lay their hands on those sheep which illuminate the characters of the two men. 'Send for some troops and teach Ghadhban a lesson,' fumed Leachman. 'You always want to be so tough,' Philby protested. Leaving Leachman, he borrowed a horse and rode off alone for a man-to-man talk with the sheikh. He seemed friendly. But the subsequent days of haggling were too much even for Philby. 'Look here, Sheikh Ghadhban,' he said at last, 'it is quite unworthy of us – you a great Arab chief and me a British Political Officer, haggling over the price of sheep. We should be exchanging worthy gifts instead of bargaining like merchants.' Within two days Ghadhban's drovers had marshalled 10,000 sheep into the army's compounds at Ali Gharbi. No blood had been shed. A decent price had been paid.

No one's pride was injured. The only sufferers were six sheep swept away in the Tigris.

An era – a long one – was ending. By 1915, twenty-six generations of Arab tribesmen had lived under Turkish domination. The Marsh Arabs, whose spirit of independence had for so long driven Turkish officials to distraction, now cautiously eyed the European newcomers. Bertram Thomas gives a good idea of the life of a British Political Officer in the Marsh area. Shatra had a terrible summer climate of 110° to 120° in the shade; cholera hung about it; the bodies of three Turkish district officers lay in the cemetery as a silent warning. Thomas was the only Englishman in a district of 130,000 tribesmen. His nearest colleagues were at Nasiriya, twenty-four miles away. 'Naturally,' he comments drily, 'speaking the local dialect of Arabic was obligatory.' Despite the heat, he revelled in the area. He noted the glory of its flora and fauna; the sudden relieving chill when the sun dips; the *mahailas* (river barges) flying their green Shia banners on the stern, carrying Arab and Persian pilgrims to Kerbela and Nejef ('the Vatican of Iraq'), their lockers below laden with corpses for burial. He took a tape measure to the *mudhif* of Sheikh Mohammed of the Albu Said and found it was 100 feet long – though Hedgcock measured one that was 8 feet longer on the Chahala. He shot duck and rode his horse. He was in seventh heaven. But quite suddenly, the British idyll in the Sumerian Garden of Eden was shattered.

The British administration in Baghdad after General Maude's entry into the capital had soon found itself struggling in a morass of political intrigue. The rulers of British India had visualized, when General Barrett's force landed at Basra, the annexation of Basra governorate. But now the idea of acquisition had burgeoned like some exotic flower. A post-war conference of the victorious Allied Powers at San Remo arbitrarily divided the Middle East into mandates for the British and French. As an outcome of dubious and undignified manoeuvres, the British secured a mandate from the League of Nations over all Iraq. (Some British officials had thought of adding the entire country to the British Empire, but the thought perished.) Iraqi intellectuals in Baghdad, Mosul and Basra, however, had made up their minds that if the Turks were expelled Iraq would become instantly and gloriously independent and republican. The Iraqis who cherished this dream – politicians, students, officers, religious divines of Nejef and Kerbela – had been considerably encouraged to develop it by the wartime play British statesmen and senior officials in Mesopotamia had made with the heady word 'self-determination'. The mandate of the British was nothing more than a crude mask for continued foreign rule. They felt promises had been broken. Bitterness mounted to volcanic proportions, and by 1920 – so soon after the euphoric days of British victory and high hopes for free Arab–British relations – the Iraqi feeling of betrayal was about to explode into a violent insurrection that for a time deprived the Baghdad administration of its control over about three-quarters of Iraq.

Gertrude Bell wrote from Baghdad in June, 1920: 'The Nationalist propaganda increases. There are constant meetings in mosques. The extremists are out for independence without Mandate. . . . They have created a reign of terror; if anyone says boo in the bazaar it shuts like an oyster. There has been practically no business done for the last fortnight.'

These were symptoms of approaching tragedy. Miss Bell wrote these words on the eve of a tribal uprising against the British that lasted from July to October 1920 and which cost the British (and Indians) – operating in shade temperatures of 110° and over – 2269 men killed, wounded and missing, and the Arabs something like 8000. The principal rising took place in the middle Euphrates area. The town of Samawa was cut off by the Beni Hacheim, Diwaniya was evacuated. The railway tracks were cut and station-masters shot. Attempting to drop stores to the Samawa garrison, a British plane was shot down and the pilot and observer killed. The gun-boat *Greenfly*, on the same mission, grounded and its British and Indian crew was captured. Several British Political Officers up and down the country were killed including Gerald Leachman, and others were hastily withdrawn from their posts (Suq-esh-Shiukh was one) to save them from the same fate.

Further north, the British suffered a murderous jolt. A column consisting of the 2nd Battalion of the Manchester Regiment, two squadrons of Scinde Horse, a battery of field artillery and a company of Sikh Pioneers was cut to pieces by tribesmen. The Manchester Column, as it came to be known, suffered nearly 200 men killed and 60 wounded, and lost 160 men as prisoners. This was the high spot of the insurrection from the Arab point of view.

In the middle Euphrates, Government had been entirely withdrawn, and the Arab tribes were delirious with success. Religious leaders in Kerbela and Nejef were preaching *jehad* against the British. The tribes of the north had responded; several isolated British officials had been killed there. The imminent risk, as the British commander-in-chief, General Sir Aylmer Haldane, knew very well, was that the Muntafiq and Tigris tribal confederations would join in the fighting. The Muntafiq, Thomas estimated, could have contributed 20,000 riflemen against the British. Thomas himself, though it looked very possible that the Gharraf tribes would rise around him, stuck it out at his post at Shatra week after week – until '200 youths were to assemble daily in front of my house to demonstrate, the tribes were carrying arms again to a man, Shia clergy were preaching *jehad*, and rifle-firing through the night became a normal practice'. At this point, when he had ceased to have any authority whatsoever, Thomas withdrew – helped to do so safely, it is important to add, by one of the powerful sheikhs who had given the British so much trouble during the war with the Turks, Sheikh Khayun al Ubaid.

In the event, by October the insurrection was over. British reinforcements were rushed in from India, raising the total of British (and Indian) forces from about 60,000 in July to about 101,000 in October. Apart from that, the Muntafiq tribes did not seriously join the revolt, although some Marsh tribes let off a volley from time to time at Euphrates river traffic. All the Tigris tribes remained passive. Even on the Gharraf, the *jehad* call did not really catch on. But for the British it had been a horribly close shave.

The reasons for the 1920 revolt against the British, and for its failure, are complex. The agitation by urban nationalists for a completely independent Iraq without the British was one factor. Added to that, a number of sheikhs genuinely believed that the British General Maude had promised on entering Baghdad that Mesopotamia would be for the Arabs. Now, they thought they saw the British digging in for a prolonged occupation. A religious factor was the hostility to the 'infidel' British presence of the Muslim divines in the holy cities, Nejef and Kerbela. Still a fourth element in the tragedy was the irritation of certain tribes at the new administrative discipline imposed by the British, and new taxes.

The Tigris tribes remained quiet partly because the grand sheikhs were satisfied with their land settlement; partly because they were geographically farthest from the influence of the religious leaders preaching *jehad*; and partly, so at least senior British officials in Baghdad thought, because of the sympathy and consideration the Amara Political officer, Captain Hedgcock, had shown for the Arabs with whom he had to deal. The Muntafiq did not rise, perhaps, because of the immense prestige of men like Khayun al Ubaid, who replied to the emissaries of the religious leaders in Nejef and to the chiefs of militant tribes that the Muntafiq had been too much weakened by internal conflict and the events of the war against the Turks to risk further disasters. This point was used by other former enemies of the British who now stood by them – men like Sheikh Ali al Fadhil and Badr al Rumaiyidh of the Albu Salih.

In the end, Thomas handed over to Sheikh Khayun before he evacuated his isolated post during the rising. Within six months he was back and remained as Political Officer for six months more, dividing his time between hunting with a pack of long-dogs and indulging an amateur's enthusiasm for archaeology. When he left Shatra, the sheikhs gave him a farewell party and handed him a souvenir. It was a sword, and they presented it saying, 'This is the sword that led us at the battle of Butaniya'.

The fighting shed light on Arab military and physical prowess. During the insurrection, British military headquarters in Baghdad issued some notes on Modern Arab Warfare for the use of their troops. 'The Arab insurgents (it said) may be met with in any number up to 10,000. One in four is usually mounted, and one in three armed with a modern rifle. The remainder represent the supply and medical services of a regular army, removing the dead and wounded. . . . They flock to the banner of their sheikh and then to the sound of the guns, moving and collecting with a rapidity little short of marvellous. Their ammunition is limited. They are consequently very careful in its use. They must be considered good shots. . . . However, owing to their lack of organization . . . they can rarely alter plans once made.'

As to the Arabs' speed of movement, an Indian cavalry officer noted in the operations round Qurna in 1915 that, when mounted, the Arab tribesmen could always outpace the British cavalry. He himself was mounted on no mean polo pony – it had been a reserve mount for the International Polo match with the United States. He found that on their own terrain the Arabs *on foot* could go faster than he could. As to the Arabs' shooting, my own observation tells me that it is not always the most accurate in the world. Yet, their bullets forced British pilots to keep 2000 feet up. And it is true that in 1926 a Muntafiq tribesman took a shot at Sir Alan Cobham's plane as he flew over on his record-breaking flight to Australia and killed the wretched mechanic at his side.

The year 1920 was a fearful one. The insurrection had cost the British Government twenty million pounds. Some British officials, Brigadier Stephen Longrigg told me recently, felt that after the revolt and bloodshed 'things never felt quite the same again'. Though law and order had returned, the bitterness of frustrated aspirations had not been exorcised. Instead of independence and a republic the Iraqis were presented with a Hashemite king, Faisal (Miss Bell's favourite), and an administration heavily reliant on British advisers. Faisal was the most famous leader in the Arab Revolt, of which T. E. Lawrence wrote in *Seven Pillars of Wisdom*. As the son of the Sharif

Hussein of the Hejaz, he was of noble desert origins, was a sympathetic, sensitive and honourable man, but he was installed in Baghdad by the British and this foreign sponsorship was never forgotten or forgiven. At Faisal's British-style coronation in 1921, Iraq became, an English writer has said, 'an Anglo-Arab kingdom,' half-way between a colony and a nation. Although gradually Iraq was to become an independent state and member of the League of Nations, and although the mandate was eventually ended, the taint of the British connection that fell on Faisal and on the son and grandson who succeeded him, as well as on many other prominent Iraqi graduates of the Arab Revolt, was never washed away. In 1958 it was to be a major cause of the violent overthrow of the monarchy.

For the moment, in 1920, however, peace and friendship returned to the Marshes; and perhaps thanks to the insurrection there was a great mutual respect between the local British Political Officers and the tribesmen. Bertram Thomas, happy to be back in the wide, green spaces of Shatra after the collective nightmare, jotted down in his notebook the following indisputable thought: 'The tribesman, with his rifle at his side and living in remote places, is governable only so long as he is convinced of his ruler's power and will to govern, *as well as of that ruler's genuine desire for his welfare.*'

6 Dreams of a Shipping Clerk

In 1951 Basra showed no trace of having been the supply-hub of great military operations in two world wars. In the Second World War its wharves and airstrips had supported the British campaign against Reza Shah of Persia and against an Iraqi nationalist rising in Baghdad. The British regiments and Gurkha battalions had long departed; but the port still flourished.

From the BOAC *Argonaut* that circled the port before landing, I saw the queue of big merchant ships waiting at anchor in the centre of the Shatt al Arab as they do today; bows pointing up-stream, equi-distant from each other like men-of-war in battle-line about to fire broadsides into the little city. Basra was then Iraq's only port, and the ships rode there taking on wheat and barley brought down from the Gharraf and Amara. The grain was loaded by sweating coolies into slings from iron barges that snuggled alongside them like piglets against a sow: 10,000 to 15,000 tonners of the Lascar-crewed British India Line, for the Bremen-based Hansa Line with big red Maltese Crosses painted on their black funnels, of the Maersk and Strick lines and a dozen other companies. I used to fancy that the clang and rasp of their winch-cables, the thudding of their donkey-engines and the metallic booming of colliding barges must be audible to Marsh Arabs in their silent reed-beds further north.

My job was to see that the cargoes of Ralli Brothers, the company I worked for, were correctly loaded, and so my days were divided between Ralli Brothers' dank, crumbling office in the old bazaar and the ships. Their steel decks were often wind-swept and slippery with rain in wintertime and always as hot as oven-tops in Basra's cruel summers, but it was good to be on the river whatever the weather. I was rowed out to the ships by the same old man and his son in their long, crude gondola-like boat (called a *bellam* in Iraq). 'Good morning,' the old man said as he fixed the heavy oars in their rowlocks. '*Al Alamani* (the German ship) today? *Al Hollandi?*'

The waters of the Shatt al Arab, the confluence of the Euphrates and Tigris, were deep here, the colour of strong coffee with milk in it, and the current strong. It flowed fast and powerfully in the straight, wide channel to the sea, but you got no feel of nearness to any sea; no salty tang penetrated up here. The port was well inland and this enhanced its beauty. For the green banks of the waterway were lined, mile after mile, with the date-palms for which southern Iraq is famous, shaking their fronds in every breeze like mops of uncombed hair: dense groves inhabited sparsely by the Arab employees of the date-exporting firms, and enlivened by kingfishers, bee-eaters, warblers and black and white crows. The Old City of Basra, full of cadaverous Arab houses with embossed wooden doors and heavy casements that tilted perilously over passers-by in the street, stood back from the Shatt al Arab. It was connected to it by a long creek which ran past the Governor's offices and then through a sprawling residential and market quarter called Ashar. On the south side of the Ashar creek a long, straight corniche borders the Shatt al Arab. There, several British employees of shipping companies and date-packing firms lived in old, ponderous Turkish mansions. From their first-floor verandas they could look down over their evening drinks and watch the big steel ships noisily winching up their cargoes, the *bellam*-men straining their oars against the current, and the motor-boats restlessly chugging back and forth. Sometimes these launches carried wedding parties, loud with thudding drums and tambourines and singing. In the hot weather the crewmen of the dhows that come up from the Gulf, or even from Zanzibar, came ashore and sprawled under the trees on the water's edge in midsummer indolence. Close to Old Basra

on the edge of the desert that stretches uninterrupted to the Red
Sea was the little town of Zubair, near where the Prophet
Mohammed's son-in-law, Ali, fought the fratricidal Battle of
the Camel. A little further north was the airstrip at Shuaiba
where the British and Indian Armies scattered the Turks and
their Arab tribal irregulars in 1915. And then the water and the
reed-beds of the Madan began and straddled the way north.

The commercial buildings of Ashar had high ceilings and old,
baroquely embellished fans that either hardly turned fast
enough to stir the heavy humid air or, if turned up too far, went
berserk and started whizzing round like aeroplane propellers,
scattering papers in all directions and threatening to tear loose
and fall spinning amongst the clerks. Not all offices had air-
conditioning: many had windows screened by light hurdles
covered with sprigs of dry, brittle thorn on to which water
dribbled from a pipe; this may have lowered the temperature
a degree or two. Basra was criss-crossed by canals and perhaps
they increased the humidity that plastered shirts to your back
like cellophane.

'The Venice of the East', someone had nick-named Basra
because of those canals. It wasn't like Venice, despite the canals,
but I think most visitors find a tranquil, sultry charm nonetheless in its corniche, in its cool, dark, sweetly odorous bazaars,
in the date-gardens that straggle up the waterway pointing a
long green finger towards the Marshes. Basra was – and is – an
important commercial centre. I don't know what the foreign
business population was then, but it must have been
considerable.

By the time I arrived in Iraq in early 1951, those usually
hard-working, Arabic-speaking and genuinely intrepid British
administrators, who were there usually because they wanted to
be, had long departed. Philby was by then an elderly man, living
in King Ibn Saud's Arabia, and famous as an explorer, cartog-
rapher and writer. Bertram Thomas, having been the first
European to cross the huge Empty Quarter of Arabia on foot
and camel-back (Philby and Thesiger were the second and third
respectively), had gone on to found the Middle East Centre for

Arab Studies (MECAS) at Shemlan in Lebanon, later to be known as a 'spy school'. Dickson was in Kuwait writing his masterly book *The Arab of the Desert*. Others, who had similarly spent part of their youth in the Iraq of the Mandate, were in other jobs or respectable retirement or had died. Iraqi officials had long since taken over their duties. Socially, the British 'pioneers' in Mesopotamia were replaced by an eager tide of British merchants, shippers, oilmen, bank managers, assessors and the like, who followed on with wives and children when things looked politically well settled. Most of these newcomers rooted themselves, naturally enough, in the cities where their offices were. They caused neat housing estates and British-only clubs to be built and planted their wives and children firmly inside them, hedging them round with reassuring protocol: visiting cards, hats and long gloves at Embassy garden parties, bridge parties, and committee work. Everything they did to 'improve' their lives separated them from the Arabs of Iraq. It was as if they deliberately set out to hack down the last bridges of sympathy that linked the British community and the Iraqis, many of whom still felt affection for Britons they had come to know in earlier, socially more relaxed days. Since 1932, Iraq had been an independent, self-administering country; a member of the League of Nations; an Arab monarchy under heavy British influence, it is true, yet independent nonetheless.

In the history of Iraqi-British relations, 1932–58 was a sad period of growing apart. It lasted through to the end of the reign of King Faisal I in 1936, survived King Ghazi, who died young in an automobile accident in 1939, and continued through the reign of his boy-son King Faisal II who ruled under the dominant eyes of his uncle, Prince Abdulillah, and his shrewd, old Prime Minister, Nuri es Said. Successive British Ambassadors, still grandly pro-consular, lorded it in the great walled embassy on the Tigris. It was an uneasy period that lasted until the revolution in 1958 swept that era away, and today, although many Britons (and other non-Arabs) work in Iraq and although even the British Club in Baghdad survives, the stuffy chauvinism of some British 'sahibs', that could be so oppressive in the Basra of the early 1950s, is no more. But even at the late date of my arrival I was in time, if only just, to glimpse the few final flickerings of the old British *raj* life that somehow survived there. Although, of course, Iraq was never part of the Empire, Kipling, perhaps even Conrad, could still have felt reasonably at home in Basra in 1951.

I remember sweating in appalling damp heat up the grubby cement steps to our little office in the heart of the bazaar, being greeted by young Salman, the tea-boy, Mr Haik, our huge but gentle Armenian accountant whose rolling, sweating chins emerged winter and summer from acres of tweed suiting and waistcoats, and our one Assyrian girl typist, whose name I wish I could remember. I introduced myself to my more senior British colleague, a nice, diminutive, middle-aged Liverpudlian who stepped forward, hand outstretched, to greet me, with perspiration flowing down the lines of his face. Another British colleague, an old stager, dressed in solar topee and knee-length bell-bottomed shorts, took me under his wing in the lunchbreak and drove me – or rather, his driver, Ali, with four gold teeth, drove us – to the British Club, a stricken-looking thatched bungalow near the Shatt al Arab waterway. The club was home-from-home to the British community.

'You'll have to join, old chap,' he said as we creaked across the club's loose verandah floorboards, and fat, splay-footed lizards flicked away from us. 'Doesn't *do* to try and live much on your own.'

As far as the leaders of the British community were concerned it evidently did not do at all. I found that out later when my craving to get into wild places and be an explorer became irresistible and I began edging away from the pleasant but limited and monotonous life of British Basra; first, spending my evenings trying to learn Arabic, later disappearing for weekends, and indeed any other holidays, up to the Marshes. Stern or pained looks of outrage began to come my way then; and soon, after a number of whiskies and sodas had gone down the hatch in the club, some old Basra hands, perhaps a Glaswegian Cargo Superintendent, grizzled by fifteen years in the Gulf, or a manager of a British bank completing his quarter century of sweltering postings from Aleppo to Abadan, would put a kindly hand on my shoulder and say, 'Look, laddie, take it easy. I've seen people go native before, you know.' Such warnings were unsettling though well-meant.

On the whole the Old Basra Hands were a boozy, warm-hearted lot, enjoying life as best they could in an uncomfortable climate, and working hard for their pensions. Some of them lived in houses that were over-grand. All had cars and servants. But for six summer months a year Basra is a cruel place to live in, even now, in a time of universal air-conditioning. If they chanced to meet them, I think most of the British of Basra liked Iraqis – it is easy to do so – though perhaps an unwieldy sense of paternalism and condescension blurred any true affection. Some Old Hands had even learned Arabic, encouraged by an annual bonus from their firms if they did so; not just kitchen Arabic but fluent Iraqi in which they transacted business at the office.

Nevertheless, to spend much time with 'the locals', leave alone tribesmen, was regarded as totally unnecessary, possibly unhealthy, and even obscurely disloyal by the bluff, pipe-smoking bosses of the big shipping and date-packing firms, the bankers, the insurance agents. Hospitable, jolly, gregarious men, they felt vaguely insulted if a newcomer showed that he could do without them and their elaborate programmes of club entertainments – the Bachelors' Balls, the St George's, St Andrew's and Burns' Nights, New Year's Eve Dances, the fancy-dress at Hallowe'en.

Their wives – the *memsahibs* – having far more time on their hands to give to considerations of status and their committees, were even more insistent on strict adherence to the Law of the British Club and Community. Outside that Law dwelt, if not lesser, at least highly dubious breeds of men. So the British matrons' social contact with Iraqis, of whom they saw few at close quarters except their servants, was virtually non-existent. In 1954, only four years before the revolution that for ever destroyed the monarchy in Baghdad, I remember a rumpus in the Club that split the small British community into two furious factions.

A young member of the Club's committee made a suggestion never made before: Why not, he daringly asked, as a gesture of goodwill, invite the Iraqi Governor of Basra and the Chief of Police – grand persons who, of course, controlled our lives since we were all licensed dwellers in their country – to look in at the New Year's Eve frolics at the Club? He might as well have thrown a thunderflash into the Club on Bridge Night. Some cried, 'Oh, come now!' and others, 'Young puppy!' And while inadequate and ancient ceiling fans stirred air as wet and heavy as damp muslin, people crowded into an Extraordinary General Meeting in the bar with its fly-specked copies of *Punch* where old Gopal, the irritable Goanese barman, poured whisky and soda with extreme ill grace. There they heard this cautious gesture of international goodwill ruled to be 'preposterous', and a stern lady denouncing it as 'a dangerous thin end of the wedge'.

So the matter rested – until four years later the revolution of 1958 transformed the question quite suddenly from whether Iraqi officials should be admitted for two hours a year to the Club into whether *any* British men and women would be allowed to remain in Iraq at all.

It was a shame, this deliberate desire of the British community to cut itself off from Iraq. It was also something that the British military and political officers who sweated in huts, tents or inadequate offices to administer the country after the expulsion of the Turks and who nearly all came to love it, would have found incomprehensible. As I described earlier, good, bad or indifferent as administrators they may have been (most seem to have been pretty competent), but these mostly middle- or upper-class Englishmen had immersed themselves in the lives and customs of Iraqis in cities, towns, villages, in mountains or on the edge of the mosquito-ridden swamps through choice and with enthusiasm. A special glow illuminates Gertrude Bell's letters when she writes home about the personal relationships with Iraqis she always sought and often attained.

But things had changed by the 1950s. I was outstandingly lucky to meet someone in Basra who was, by then, an exception – though he would not have been perhaps thirty years earlier – to the general run of foreigners.

As I have said, Wilfred Thesiger is made from the formidable mould of Richard Burton, Gertrude Bell and Charles Doughty. I have briefly described his wandering life before I met him. Immediately before coming to Basra he had spent a season or two with the Kurds. Then he journeyed south. It seems incredible now that, if he had not, my life might have side-slipped the Marsh Arabs who are now my friends and I might never have known the enchantment of their rough and ready paradise.

The *sahibs* of the British community watched askance Thesiger's tall, lanky figure (and later my own) striding about the *suqs* of Basra on the rare occasions he went there to buy supplies or medicines. They raised disbelieving eyebrows at the two or three long-cloaked and rather grubby Marsh Arabs flip-flopping in sandals beside him; they were deeply perplexed. In their eyes Thesiger was clearly an eccentric, yet they couldn't help respecting him for his brilliant war record, with General Orde Wingate in Abyssinia and with Special Air Service behind the German lines in the Libyan Desert, and for his DSO. Once Thesiger lectured on the Marsh Arabs at the British Club and people were cautiously interested.

Far from making light of the discomforts of the Marshes – the dirty water, the cheek-by-jowl communal living, the sweat, the fleas – Thesiger gave it to them straight, and you could see their bewildered disapproval of our sort of life. 'Why don't you

do something *useful?*' a nice bank manager said to me, a man who, oddly enough, apart from being a jovial pillar of the Club and the (all-British) Basra Amateur Dramatic Society, enjoyed travel books and admired eccentrics like Orde Wingate (although *he* was a *soldier* which, I suppose lent him an officially sanctioned and therefore acceptable eccentricity.) 'You mean, like becoming a bank manager?' I asked irritably. 'Well . . . yes,' he said.

When, later, I had visited the Marshes once or twice, Marsh Arab friends regularly came down to Basra to see me at home. They came from Mejar squeezed into the crowded, ramshackle buses with the springs sticking painfully out of the seats, braving a strange city and rude townsmen, clutching presents for me of eggs wrapped in little baskets made of raffia, or even a scrawny chicken or two, their eyes glazed from being dangled head down for several hours in the heat. Suddenly oddly pathetic figures out of their own environment – in which they assumed a striking dignity and great natural grace – they appeared grinning on the steps of my Basra shipping office, to the quiet amusement of the astonished clerks.

My Greek boss, George Pavlides, a rough and ready but humane and sensible man, took to them at once; he would lead them in and sit them down in our tearoom and tell Salman, the tea-boy, to get a move on and start brewing up. Sometimes, if the office was closed, I would hear tapping at the window of my small house and look up to see two or three figures in off-white *dishdashas*, black and white headcloths and flimsy black or brown cloaks peering anxiously to see if I was there. If I was out and the cook, who had orders to let them in at any time of day or night, was also away in the bazaar, they would settle down on their haunches on the front doorstep and calmly wait for me to return. I had no beds for them, but they curled up happily on rugs on the floor; and as soon as he saw them Jassim, my good-natured cook, would hurry unbidden to the market to buy food for them if we were short.

Now and again, of course, someone else would come to call – an acquaintance in one of the British trading companies or a date-packing firm, or worse still a British wife – and find these friendly, innocent Arabs grinning and chittering at them from the doorstep. After encounters like that, the furtive or accusing glances in my direction on Club Nights would multiply: I was obviously 'going native'.

Luckily for my morale, in the British Consulate-General things were different. There we had the amused understanding of the Consul, the late Mark Kerr-Pearse, whose luncheon invitation had led to Wilfred Thesiger's casual but, for me, momentous remark, 'I'll be back in six weeks for a bath. Why not come up for a week in the Marshes then?' – and so to my stepping ashore from the great war-canoe in the shadow of Sheikh Falih's *mudhif* on that sun-bathed day in 1952. The arched entrance of that *mudhif* had been Thesiger's gateway to the Marshes, as it was to be mine. And, as it happened, that particular gateway very soon ceased to exist.

7 The Last of the Sheikhs

As the early 1950s saw the last flickerings of British *raj* attitudes in Iraq, so they saw the twilight of the great tribal sheikhs of the south. The first of the sheikhs I met in Iraq, as I have said, was Sheikh Falih bin Majid el Khalifa. Thesiger had made friends with him a year or two before and Falih, though at first baffled by Thesiger's longing to actually plunge in amongst the Marsh Arabs and suffer the flies and fleas and heat, had good-naturedly lent him the canoe and canoe-men with which to do so. The first real Marsh Arabs, therefore, that Thesiger (and later I myself) encountered, were Falih's vassals. From time to time, Falih himself liked to hunt the monstrous wild boars and shoot the wildfowl that teem in the marshes, but he would never have spent more time than absolutely necessary there, and shuddered at the thought of staying the night in a Marshman's house.

I was only to know Falih a very short time. The following year he was killed by a careless nephew in a shooting accident. After my first visit with Thesiger I, too, stayed in Falih's guesthouse and benefited from his enormous hospitality, and went pig-shooting with him. After his death I was entertained in the same *mudhif* by his son, Abdel Wahed. Though Falih could deal harshly with disobedience, he was in many ways an admirable man. When he died, Amara and Sabaiti, Thesiger's boatmen, wept; and Falih's name awoke respect and regret from Nasiriya to the eastern Marshes. And that thought leads me to say something about sheikhs of southern Iraq in general, many of whom where not admirable at all at that period but little despots straddling land which, with its periodic droughts and floods, was a hard enough taskmaster in itself for those who worked it. The word 'sheikh' has been translated 'lord of the manor' and 'squire', but both expressions are misleading. The tribes of southern Iraq, including the Madan, were, and are, closely related to the nomadic tribes in their black tents east of the Euphrates. They cherish the traditions of the desert Arabs. So the sheikhs were merely the first among equals. Chosen by common consent, sheikhs were accepted and respected only as long as they effectively shouldered their responsibility for the well-being of the tribe in peace and for leading it into battle in war. A sheikh's title could be transferred and tribesmen would desert an unsatisfactory sheikh for another of his family. These natural aristocrats – through in-breeding their blood was the purest in the Arab world – followed a democratic code. The influx of these thoroughbred tribesmen into southern Iraq over the centuries and their co-mingling with the already resident cultivators meant that this code had taken sturdy root there. The peoples in and on the edge of the Marshes had entirely adopted it. The early twentieth century war-leaders, Saihud of the Albu Mohammed and Ibn Madhkur of the Beni Lam, were two examples of tribal leaders in the Amara area who were regarded, and behaved, according to immemorial Arab tribal tradition.

Bertram Thomas describes how in his day one had to address an important sheikh in the baroque phrases evolved by oriental protocol:

'O Sheikh Mohammed, you know that Government is strong to punish wrong-doing, and generous to reward faithful service?'

'Government is a father. First Allah, then the Hukuma (Government).'

'Well said, O Sheikh! But a father is angered with a slothful or unwilling son.'

'God destroy the house of the father of sloth.'

'I have come to you in the Hukuma's name. Government has need of 200 men of the Beni Said, and wants them today.'

'I kiss your hand, but. . . .' And so on, for perhaps an hour or two.

The war-canoes – the *taradas* – such as the one in which I arrived at Falih's house, symbolize heroic days of major tribal warfare in southern Iraq. Days of tough, flamboyant but in some sense popular leadership; days of great bloodshed that began to dwindle in ferocity after the First World War. The tribes learned a grim lesson from the long struggle between the Albu Mohammed and the Beni Lam in the late nineteenth and early twentieth century. It was like the Hundred Years War between England and France in miniature. Year after year, the sheikhs planted their war-flags at their *mudhif* doors and sent messengers to call in the tribesmen for battle. It is said that 10,000 died. This figure may be an exaggeration, but undeniably hundreds were killed before Saihud and Ibn Madhkur wisely put a stop to the mutual slaughter of their tribes.

Blood feud and killing still occur in the Marshes as we shall see later on, but on a lesser scale, I should think, than the violent crime rate of London or New York. In any case it is utterly insignificant in comparison to the great battles of the past that involved sometimes hundreds, perhaps even thousands, of men. An old man of the once war-going Albu Mohammed confederation of tribes was right when he said, half-mockingly, of his own people today, 'Their swords have become swords of lead; they glitter but cut not.' And wars, more than peace, produce leaders who lead.

For all this, even in the 1950s I found simple, hard-working sheikhs among the Madan, chosen only for their personal quality; and these dutiful men received few rewards for their pains and indeed were often quite poor. But the successors to the great Saihud had often degenerated into mere feudal landlords who made personal fortunes from vast estates, lived on the dry land in forts of concrete houses, and probably owned a large American limousine and a mansion in Baghdad. Their powerful presences loomed over the region casting as great a shadow over those who lived there as the government itself. In fact, they often treated government officials as if they were

there to be ignored. Now and again, it is true, tribesmen preferred – and who can blame them – to risk local justice and punishment by unsatisfactory sheikhs in familiar surroundings to undergoing an often Kafka-esque experience in government police stations or jails amongst contemptuous strangers. But still, in pre-1958 days, tribesmen were utterly at the mercy of too many extortionate bullies with gold braid on their robes extending hands to be subserviently kissed. They were one reason for serious, large-scale emigration of land-labourers from the Amara area to the imagined Eldorados of Baghdad and Basra in the early 1950s, an exodus that threatened a dangerous setback in agricultural production in a nation largely dependent on it.

In theory, all land belonged to the Iraqi State, but only in theory. The fact was that land-owning sheikhs in southern Iraq had been able to lease great tracts from the government and had then proceeded to run them with as much bare-faced confidence as if they owned them by right. Most of these lands were cultivable, but some fiefdoms spilled over into the permanent Marshes and enveloped purely Madan villages and the Madan tribes that inhabited them. Falih's father, Majid, was master of one of these sprawling fiefdoms and one of the two paramount sheikhs of the Albu Mohammed tribes near Amara. I met him only once. He waddled into Falih's *mudhif* one day, a sweating, cross old man, with eyes too small and a midriff too gross, barking orders to a small crowd of terrified attendants and slaves. He lowered himself to the ground with difficulty as if – as many did in this region of water and humidity – he suffered from rheumatism as well as sheer gluttony. He asked me if I could arrange to sell him a smart, modern launch that would run him up and down the Tigris. When I said I couldn't, he lost interest in me. Soon the *mudhif* was alive with chatter and people bustling in and out – bringing accounts, and men reporting on the state of the crops or a problem of irrigation or the need for more water-pumps, and a host of petitioners of one sort or another. Majid was not a permanently absent landlord as others were.

Majid was a millionaire and his tribesmen could be better described by then as peasant labourers, working desperately hard for a precarious and certainly none too generous share of the sheikh's crop of rice or winter wheat and barley. Majid was therefore no longer a traditional kind of sheikh, but simply a feudal landlord. Of course, it was in his interest to be an efficient landlord, to see that each parched acre received its quota of water – although not all landlords, some of them notoriously absentee, did even that. But the security of his share-cropping labourers, and their wives and many children, depended to a very great extent on the whim of this rheumatic old curmudgeon who spent very little time pondering their welfare. Thesiger, in his book on the Marshes, recalls Majid's anguished cry at the mourning for Falih, his son, 'My land! Now, when I die, what will happen to my land?' And Thesiger comments dryly, 'I thought it sad at the time that he put his land before his people.'

Perhaps young King Faisal's ministers in Baghdad saw the sheikhs as a safeguard for the régime – the King himself, a sophisticated youth, educated at Harrow School in England, would hardly have felt much at ease with people like Majid. Majid's tribe numbered about 120,000 which meant he could mobilize, say, 25,000 armed men on the instant: a sizeable force. Furthermore, the city of Amara at that time was thought to be politically unstable – it was leftist, largely in reaction to the surrounding feudalism. So the government may have thought that such a private army was a useful weapon lying so close to such a potential political trouble spot. Whatever else, Majid would certainly have done his best to uphold the monarchy.

The Albu Mohammed villages were dotted along the irrigated, or flooded, lands on the Tigris and the tributaries of it which meandered into the Marshes. The people were *fellahin* (peasants), for the most part, not Madan. But Falih and Majid claimed ruler's right over real Madan villages too, rights that obliged the inhabitants to hand over a share of the rice crops, and provide reeds and labour for the sheikhs on pain of beating or fines. Their headmen were responsible for prompt delivery of whatever was ordered.

One of these headmen, a sturdy, friendly Marshman, called Sahain, which means 'little dish', became a particular friend and has remained my friend to this day. His ragged village of reed houses 'in the belly of the Marsh', as the Madan expression goes, became a kind of home from home for Thesiger and myself. His younger brother, Hafadh, often travelled with me through the Marshes and once or twice stayed with me in Basra to shop or be taken to the doctor.

People like Sahain and Hafadh knew little first-hand of the usual relations between sheikh and tribesmen – the mutual respect and sense of interdependence that in the great tradition of Arabia exists between even the strongest sheikhs and their people. Endless stories circulated amongst the Marsh Arabs of injustices by sheikhs and their representatives, of extortion by outlying bailiffs, of floggings and fines. I recall being told one

such story at Sahain's, how a neighbouring sheikh of brutal
reputation was addicted to popping people who annoyed him
into a coffin-shaped box full of nails; he ordered his servants to
throw the box around until the victim emerged battered and
bleeding. This sadist may have been the same infamous sheikh
of whom the Madan, who love music and dancing, sometimes
sang, mocking the evil memory, round their evening fires.

> 'The Arabs told me of him,
> A tryant from an early age. . . .'

When I returned in the sheikh-less 1970s, I began one day to
murmur these almost forgotten words at Sahain's crowded
house and at once people laughed, 'Good God, he remembers
that!' – and they started up the song again, the older men
explaining to the younger ones what it was all about. Naturally
not all sheikhs behaved like little Jenghis Khans. Falih, for
example, was a son of the awesome Majid, but his tribesmen
regarded him quite differently. He was tough, all right, and
proudly aware of his power and position. He expected immediate obedience and could be harsh if he didn't get it. Most
important, Falih was not pompous and stand-offish. He was
hospitable; he was available; he listened. He bandied jokes with
villagers and tribesmen; he dropped in on the Madan whom
some people of his class despised. He was not afraid, as we
might say, to get his hands dirty. He had a reputation as an
excellent horseman, shot well and could even handle a Marshman's wobbly canoe.

There were other sheikhs more gentle and born to lead. One
I know, Maziad bin Hamdan of the Al Isa, a shepherd tribe on
the northern edge of the Marshes, lost a small fortune out of
his own pocket trying to improve his tribe's crop production.
A sign of the times: he now spends half the year running a small
hotel in Basra. Another sheikh, an almost saintly old figure,
Jasim bin Faris of the Fartus tribe deep in the Marshes, was a
gossamer scrap of a man always puffing at a cigarette-holder,
who worked and guided and led his people with a voice not

much more emphatic than a whisper. He survived the purges of the revolution and was still sheikh of the Fartus up to his death in 1976 – at heaven knows what age – to the satisfaction of all concerned.

But an era died when the monarchy perished. As the post *raj* British disappeared so did the sheikhly landlords of the Marsh world. From the abortive upheaval of 1920 and the subsequent imposition of the monarchy by the British to the late 1950s, nationalism had proliferated in the Kingdom like a strong creeper grappling a wall. By 1958 the wall was ready to fall, and did so. The collapse buried not only the royal family and those close to the palace, but merchants, too, and politicians and land-owners. Pompous sheikhs were banished from their lands to easy exile in Baghdad where they live comfortably but without power.

So the fiefdom that Majid feared for in the hour of his son's death passed into other hands – the hands in fact of Majid's own tribesmen, now at last landowners in their own right. Perhaps Falih died in good time, before his familiar world disintegrated. The great *mudhif* with its eleven reed arches and 60 feet of length is no more. Not a stone remains of the house that stood just behind it where Falih, the family that survived him (living quietly in Baghdad now) and his servants and guards (dispersed to city jobs, or jobs in the police or the army) once lived. The ridged land, once Falih's own, stretches up to Wadiya waterway uninterrupted these days by any human habitation until where old Sayyid Sarwat holds majestic, but entirely spiritual court, like some wise old man of another time. And so, the place where I first set foot thirty years ago on the threshold of the Marshes, is now green, silent and empty.

8 *The World of the Marshes*

'*Hadha el hor!*,' Hafadh cried from the *tarada*'s stern. 'This is the Marsh.' He leaned across his paddle and squeezed my shoulder as if to add, 'This is *our* world, you understand. You are in *our* hands now!' Thesiger, fitting cartridges into a shotgun, looked up – 'Yes, this is it.' The breeze was light and cool. Soft white clouds moved across the blue sky. It was a fine winter's day in the Marshes like countless others I was to see in the years to come. The difference was that this was my first day. A moment ago the palisade of reeds had risen behind us, cutting us off with apparent finality from the outside world, even from Sheikh Falih's *mudhif* and Sayyid Sarwat's voice booming a welcome. In their element once more, our four canoe-boys settled back, chattering to each other, relaxed. Their paddles dipped and rose more languidly trailing tinkling liquid drops back into the water.

These canoe-boys were typical Madan: Hafadh, Ajram, Hasan and Yasin. If I could draw I think I would be able to catch their likenesses accurately after more than twenty years. I jotted down a few notes on their appearances at the time:

Ajram: angled, bony profile – prominent temples and cheekbones. Very wide mouth, fair skin. Big bony hands: light hairs, no moustache. Already deepening furrows of laughter bracket the corners of his mouth. No beauty, but good-hearted and never grumbles. Grins easily and means it.

Hasan bin Muhaisin: square face, short straight nose. Deep-set, widely spaced eyes and black eyebrows. Very white, level teeth. Solemn expression. Tentative smile. Slow of speech. Dogged.

Yasin: noticeably mongol face, high cheek-bones, up-tilted eyes; curving sensual lips; skin darker than usual; black hair, heavy hair on arms and legs and wisps of moustache. Surprisingly resonant, deep-chested voice too often raised in acrimony. Very strong and big-limbed.

Hafadh: vivacious, full mouth and a satyr's nose sweeping down to meet it. Brown hair, large, mischievous brown eyes, and good teeth and a tongue always darting between them. He looks like a wiry, brown, good-natured faun.

They were all young, zestful and alert; full of humour, some of it ribald; full of mischief usually kept in check by their natural poise, the tribesman's sense of what is fitting. They were poor – less poor than their fathers and grandfathers in Turkish times, but poorer than they are today. To wear, they owned little more than the shirts (of cotton, no longer the coarse sackcloth of Keppel's visit), the headcloths (*kafiyahs*) and headropes (*agals*), and the belts and daggers they wore every day. Despite this, appearance was important to them. When we approached a village after the antics, songs, and sweat, possibly dangers, of a long day's travelling, the boys laid down their paddles, scooped up water to wash their hands and faces, rolled down their sleeves and carefully straightened their *kafiyahs* and *agals*, peering into tiny, round mirrors to make sure they looked at their best. Sometimes one of them would thrust a comb into my hand and point to my untidy hair – a friendly hint that if one of us looked scruffy we all lost face. If our night's lodging was simple, like well-brought-up boys in Europe or America, they would automatically jump up to help our short-handed host with dishes or the coffee. At the other end of the social scale, in a sheikh's *mudhif*, those spritely Marsh yokels quietly took a humble seat in the throng with as much dignity as if they were themselves sons of sheikhs.

At such times, I thought: Can they really be descendants of those tangled-haired marauders who frightened della Valle into shifting camps to avoid them? They could be, and were. And they were grandsons and great-great-grandsons of the fierce harriers of British and Indian regiments, of the giggling men and women who were so delighted when Mr Fraser sketched them in 1834, of those untamed people who had preyed on the sumptuous caravans of ancient Greeks, Persians and Turks. These boys were proud of that kinship and of their tribes and – though Iraqi townsmen scoffed at them – proud to be Madan.

It was strange – unheard of, in fact – for outsiders like us to spend so much time, to live as the Madan did, in the heart of the Marshes. No one had ever done so before. Not surprisingly, the Madan tribesmen Thesiger first met took a very long, careful look at him before they were convinced he was harmless. Once they were satisfied, they bestowed upon him – and later, myself – the compliment of their affection.

We dawdled through the reed-lanes that first day; then struck across Dima, one of the larger lakes. In the middle of the lake, several *bellams* lay close together and a cluster of naked and half-naked men struggled half in and half out of the water with what looked like acres of netting.

'Those people are called *Berbera*,' said Ajram. 'They spend their lives catching and selling fish. They use nets which is a thing we Madan never do. Shall we buy a fish off them?'

'Why don't you use nets? It would be easier.'

'We use spears to catch fish, not nets,' Hasan called out.

'Yes, but why?'

'Don't know why. We just do. Shall we buy a fish?'

Netting fish was indeed taboo to the tribesmen in those days – like trading, it was simply 'not done'. So, the Madan fished laboriously with long bamboo spears; the spear-heads had five metal prongs with barbed tips. They also scattered bait impregnated with digitalis which paralysed the fish so that they floated unconscious to the surface and were effortlessly scooped up.

Now, a man's voice suddenly quavered up into the limitless sky.

'Your skin white and fair, as white as buttercups (it sang), your eyes like the wide eyes of the gazelle, teeth shining like stars, how will you know that I am here fainting for love as a warrior faints when he is struck by a bullet?'

Hafadh took the opportunity to blow his nose – he arched his left palm above the bridge of it and, extending the little finger like a maiden aunt holding a teacup, pinched his nostrils genteelly with thumb and forefinger and gave a sharp snort. He dipped his hand into the water to wash it, and resumed his paddling.

Echoes of the song hung in the air. But our companions were not in a sentimental mood.

'How will she know you're there?' Ajram shouted. 'Who couldn't know with that appalling racket you're making?'

And Yasin yelled, 'Come here. I'll give you something up the backside that'll make you faint.' A pause; and an embarrassed voice in the reeds said faintly, 'Oh, go away.'

At the end of the day we came to Mugheifat, Sahain's small village. It was deep in the Marshes. Sahain was Hafadh's big brother; he must have been older by seventeen or eighteen years. He was the hereditary headman, the *qalit*, of the Feraigat tribe in these parts. He was short and strong, calm and sensible. A good man, a Victorian writer would have said, 'in a tight corner'. When I saw him laughing on the threshold of his island-house, it was my first sight of a man who has remained my friend to this day. Of course, he was delighted to see Hafadh back again. But whenever Hafadh left home, as he frequently did, to accompany me round the Marshes for weeks on end or to come to Basra, Sahain was pleased with that too. If Hafadh was happy, Sahain was content. We both knew Hafadh was very happy travelling.

Hafadh was a good boatman, a fair shot, cheerful and reliable; he got on well with the others, too – an important point. Whenever we arrived at Sahain's house, he and Hafadh made it seem like my home-coming. Sahain's house was simple, the

whole insignificant village was simple – a prototypical Marsh village. You ducked into the house through what was little more than a crack in the reed wall – nothing at all like Sheikh Falih's great arched doorway. One's bare feet brushed across green rushes and reed matting on the floor. A reed screen, coming half-way up the wall towards the far end, separated off the women's quarters and the kitchen; smoke seeped up over it and hung like a fog in the curve of the ceiling. Sacks of rice and grain, paddles, fishing-spears, tattered bolsters, mattresses with the stuffing leaking out, a dilapidated dark wooden chest with a hinge missing; that, apart from the hens and cats darting among us, was all the visible content of the house, except for another much smaller box also made of wood.

From this, as soon as we arrived, Hafadh took out narrow-waisted glasses about 2 inches high which he placed on a cheap metal tray. He dipped an old black kettle into the water from the buffalo-platform, not bothering to disperse the surface scum, and placed it on the fire of reeds and dung that Sahain had already prepared in the middle of the floor. Then he broke small lumps of sugar from a large solid cone and dropped one piece into each glass. The boiling water he poured onto a handful of tea already in the pot, and put the pot onto the fire to brew. When he was satisfied with the brewing he poured the tea into the glasses. A sheikh would have produced diminutive spoons. At Sahain's you stirred your tea with short splinters of reed that you broke off the matting. Sometimes tea was replaced by pieces of dried limes which made a delicious sweet drink. In summer – in the terrible wet heat of summer – there were sometimes tall glasses of sherbert looking deliciously cool, but often luke-warm because, of course, there was no ice.

In summer, too, there was swimming; a blessed relief from the furnace of the air. The side-flaps of the houses were raised to let the breeze in: but often there was no breeze. You just sat and let the sweat run down your chest and back, and did your best to breathe air like steam from a hot bath, while you beat off the flies and mosquitoes that attacked you from above and the fleas and other insects that crept up on you from below. If you could stay there then for more than a day it meant that you really loved the Marshes.

Fortunately, the Marsh water stayed cool and deep. Doctors would have warned against bilharzia, the disease that hatches in snails which infect the standing waters. But it was sometimes too hot to worry about bilharzia. All Marsh Arabs swim like frogs from a very early age. Throwing off their ragged shirts they jumped into the water as though it was their true element. Watching them I remembered the First World War stories of Marsh Arabs; how they stripped and oiled their bodies to make capture more difficult, before slipping into the Tigris to raid a British army barge-train under the eyes of its Indian sepoy guards. I also remember the Hon. George Keppel's description in 1824 of a boatman who would have made 'an excellent model for an Hercules'.

Infant mortality among the Madan in those days was high: only the strong survived. So these Feraigat tribesmen, though slim, were enormously powerful. How could they not be? Every day of their lives they laboured at a paddle or a punt-pole, plunged about in water after buffaloes or fish or wildfowl, wielding a sickle hour after hour to cut rushes for fodder and giant reeds for building or sale.

I am not sure that I have ever met men with such power in their fingers and wrists. I think they could snap a man's neck in a trice. Their hands are wide, large-pored and hard-palmed. Often these hands are strangely hairless and they are dark skinned from the sun, about the colour of dark treacle. Their arms and bodies are several shades lighter and the skin surprisingly soft. Early travellers used the word 'shaggy' to describe Marsh Arabs, as though they were coated all over with hair, like monkeys. On the contrary, their bodies, except for the forearms and calves, are remarkably hairless. Their feet are colossal: unusually broad and thick, like bedouin feet, but deeply scarred and fissured from the ceaseless contact with decks of *mashhufs* and the daily slashes and stabs of the undergrowth of the reed-beds – rushes with edges as sharp as razors, and jagged reed-stubble thrusting up like bayonets. The Marshmen, when I first saw them, wore their hair cropped short, as they do now. Then, as now, most of them eventually grew moustaches; and some, like Sahain, affected a stubbly chinbeard. The days of plaits and ringlets have gone. Blond hair is quite common in the Marshes, and you see startlingly green or blue eyes among the black and brown.

On summer days, howling and hooting with animal glee, the younger males of the village plunged their flat-bellied circumcised bodies into the water and their sun-darkened arms and legs thrashed up the spray. It was like a carnival time. The shrieks and laughter excited the buffaloes into an orgy of groans and the dogs became hysterical and plunged in too. The women and girls, spruced up in bright dresses of scarlet, green and blue, giggling and feigning bashfulness, eagerly peered out of their doorways at all this high-spirited nakedness as if they had never seen such a thing before.

The village sits in a clearing in the reeds. But the reed-walls hedge it round quite closely. Suppose your tribe was attacking the village; with strong oarsmen and complete surprise, you could storm the first house before its inhabitants had time to get off more than a hurried shot or two. But probably some small sound borne before you on the wind would have given an earlier warning.

Between the houses, tiny boys pole themselves confidently

about on tiny, home-made rafts or in small boats called *chala-biyas*. You see buffaloes grunting and munching at the house doors, swinging their great heavy horns to ward off the persistent swarms of flies; cattle egrets perched on the curving mat roofs, black and white kingfishers hovering to sight their prey and then dropping like stones in the water. You hear the chorus of frogs. You smell the delicate evening smell of fires and the rich smell of coffee-making that brings the saliva into your mouth. You tie up the canoe, step ashore, kick off your shoes and squeeze through the narrow entrance of the house. You take a place against one of the longest walls and when, one by one, everyone sitting there gives you the greeting 'Good evening' you murmur it back to each man in turn.

A man is making coffee – the women are busy cooking behind the partition and you hear conversation there and the clash of pans and the crying of babies. The man sits cross-legged by the fire in the middle of the floor near the door. He has made the fire by igniting the end of a slim bundle of dry weeds with a cigarette-lighter and piling thin, biscuit-like pats of buffalo-dung around the burning reeds. He may add a drop or two of paraffin to encourage the flames. He puts a skillet on this fire and throws into it a handful of coffee beans. He keeps shaking the skillet and stirring the beans until they are roasted. He tips them into a metal mortar and begins to pound them with a brass pestle. The coffee is poured from a pot with a long, curved spout like a beak. At humble Bu Mugheifat you would only expect to see one such pot, not very large. In a sheikh's *mudhif* there would be an array of pots ranging from an immense, portly king-pot, 3 feet high, called a *gum-gum*, to a rank of pawnlike pots only 9 inches high called *dalla*.

A small reed structure with a white flag attached to a reed wand floating over it was the village store. Tea, coffee, spices, tobacco in tins, onions, needles, cucumbers, dates were to be found here. Perhaps mantles, too, for the pressure lamps; perhaps combs, mirrors, sugar in big cones, and salt and pepper. If the shop did not stock these goods, the villagers' infrequent visits to the markets outside the Marshes would supply them. Or now and again a peripatetic pedlar paddled a small *mashhuf*, his floating shop, through the village. Their other requirements they could supply themselves – reeds for houses, matting, and fuel; reeds for ropes and baskets; rushes for fodder. They provided their own food, too, in the main: milk and curds came from their buffaloes, fish from the lagoons, rice and wheat flour from the local cultivators.

Even in the 1950s it was not realistic to classify Madan simply as people who bred buffaloes, fished the Marshes and had no other activities. Their neighbouring tribes, the Albu Mohammed, for instance, were cultivators of land as well as buffalo-owners; the Feraigat were undoubtedly Madan but owned some rice fields as well as breeding buffaloes. Apart from those two categories, there were others who owned no cultivation whatsoever, only a few buffaloes: these poor people, too, were Madan.

All Marsh women wear ornaments, often of delicate or well-worked design. Some of these bracelets, anklets, rings and head-decorations are silver and are made by the Sabaeans, or Subba, whose religion is nearer Manichaeism than anything else (although often they are mistakenly called Christians of St John). Layard has an interesting account of them from his journey in 1840: 'Met a Sabaean (or Mandean) – or Christian of St John – an ancient sect. They went from encampment to encampment making and repairing the gold and silver ornaments worn by the women. A useful people, well treated by Arabs, but shamefully oppressed by the Turkish and Persian authorities, both to compel them to embrace Mohammedanism and to extort money from them.' The sect, in Layard's time, was thus reduced to about three or four hundred families speaking Arabic, writing Aramaic or Mandean and retaining their ancient faith. They lived in Basra and alongside the Shatt al Arab, in Qurna, Amara and Suq-esh-Shiukh. They are a handsome people and customarily heavily bearded. In those days, Muslims would not eat with them, leave alone marry into them. Last year in Baghdad I heard of a Muslim boy who had just become engaged to a Sabaean girl: both were students at Baghdad University.

I acquired a *tarada* of my own, almost as big as Wilfred's and with the same number of large iron-bossed nails studding its flanks – the nails that proclaim the craft is a *tarada*, not simply a grand *mashhuf*. Sometimes Wilfred and I joined forces to travel together. I took on Hasan bin Muhaisin, Ajram and Hafadh as canoe-men and added Chethir, another young Feraigi. Yasin went off to be married and Wilfred acquired a new crew including two cheerful and self-contained young men called Amara and Sabaiti; the first almost too perfectly and classically Arab in the features to be credible, the latter big-eyed, stubby and irrepressibly good-humoured – a neo-Sumerian, I thought.

There were days of travel and hours of Thesiger's doctoring. The Madan hardly ever saw a doctor in those times. Thesiger did what he could with a big medicine-chest, a hypodermic syringe, some training and infinite patience. At every village we were surrounded, almost overwhelmed, by what seemed like the entire local population, jostling, shouting, thrusting small children and babies towards Thesiger as he crouched, in the dim heat of a hut at evening or on a sun-drenched buffalo-platform humming with flies, injecting penicillin, handing out aspirins and cures for dysentery, constipation or eczema, and antiseptics, ointments and bandages for the hideous gashes caused by wild pigs, circumcising the infants, fending off the over-importunate.

Here, Amara came fully into his own. He fetched and carried indefatigably; competent, compassionate, handing over plaster and scissors, arranging for hot water, carefully counting out the pills from their bottles, keeping an eye open for theft. Occasionally in the heat of a minor operation, Thesiger's voice rose above the human hubbub. 'Amara, where's the iodine, damn and blast it! Oh, you bloody boy!' But afterwards there were no hard feelings, because Amara loved Thesiger.

Dysentery was endemic in the Marshes then. So was bilharzia. Its parasites infiltrate into the bloodstream and thence throughout the body and particularly into the pelvic region causing havoc and great pain. I remember seeing men with bursting, oozing sores, caused by the non-venereal version of syphilis called yaws, that I found too appalling to look at for very long but which responded miraculously to the penicillin injections. There was hookworm, too, and a great many eye afflictions, and tuberculosis, and gun-shot wounds and reed slashes and a variety of other horrors. I, too, began to take medicines with me. I could not do as much as Thesiger. But even the basic things were welcome and I could return the tribesmen's hospitality by doctoring, and by shooting the terrible pigs.

The days with Thesiger went by. My first visit to the Marshes ended. After a few weeks I returned for another spell without him.

9 Two Marriages, and a Decision

Presently, Ajram was married at Bu Mugheifat, but this did not stop him travelling with me. When his first son was born, he made me go with him to his tiny house, took the baby in its pink-swaddling clothes from its mother and thrust it, screaming, into my arms.

'Here,' Ajram said. 'This is your nephew.'

'What will you call him?'

'We call him Kharaibat,' Ajram grinned. '*Mister* Kharaibat, because of you!'

'He's going to be a good singer by the sound of him.' But Mister Kharaibat died quite soon. Ajram went on to have several more sons, some of whom died and some of whom lived. He was very poor then: only one buffalo stood at his door. It was not very big, but too big to enter the little house.

The ups and down of Ajram's existence were shared with his wife. She was a typical woman of the Marshes. The life of a Marsh woman is a segregated one and, at the same time, remarkably free. In a guest-house, their place is the other side of the mat screen which divides it. They will not intrude into the men's side except to carry in a dish of food or to bring a sick baby to be treated. Of course, in their own homes they can roam wherever they like – it is theirs as much as their husband's.

The women are certainly not the down-trodden slaves, despised, ignored and over-worked that, I suppose, many Europeans imagine them to be. They work, it is true: but so do the men; work is the lot of every human being in the Marshes. You see women punting canoes to the market. You see them sitting

on the platforms outside their houses, chatting happily, shouting jokes to passing male villagers, and even an occasional
obscene remark which the men will reply to with a laugh. Umm
Warid, Sahain's wife and the mother of his eldest son, Warid,
talks to me quite naturally – it is like talking to any mother in
London. If there are no strangers there, she crosses into the
men's part of Sahain's house, and sits with us for a time
gossiping and laughing. She has an exceptionally strong, fine
face; not, as I write, any longer beautiful (I remember her
beauty those years ago when her brother-in-law Hafadh showed
her to me with a proud nudge of his elbow), but strong, and
firm-mouthed with clear, shrewd, honest eyes. When Sahain is
there, too, you can see that, out of tradition – but also, I think,
out of a genuine love and respect – she gives him gladly the
leading role in the house; one could hardly expect her to do
anything else. But he allows her her say, too. And she has it,
boldly giving sound advice, outspokenly chiding a tribesman
who has said something silly or unkind; ending a session of talk
with a brusque 'Well, dinner is ready now!' I go and sit with
her sometimes as she and her daughters knead bread and pluck
a fowl at the back door of Sahain's house. We talk of Warid's
future, of places I have seen, or how to cook a heron (boil it for
forty-eight hours) or breast of cormorant (she knows my
opinion: have nothing to do with it).

   If someone paddles me slowly through the village, it is like a
stroll down a familiar village street in England. The women are
out-of-doors, pounding reeds for matting, pounding coffee,
washing babies, chasing dogs out of the food store, shouting
instructions to children poling away into the reeds. Their voices
ring clear across the clear expanses of water.

   'Good morning!'

   'Good morning. How are you?'

   'Good morning, Umm Shibil!' I call back. 'How's Haji's back
today? Has Khanjar gone to school yet, Arafa? Saddam's diar-
rhoea is still bad? – all right, I'll bring some pills in a little while.
Umm Hasan, tell your son Wawi we shall start out to look for

geese just before sunset. He should come to Sahain's in good time or he'll be left behind.'

It is not easy to generalize a woman's life. It is so varied and contradictory in its social implications. Women tend the kitchens; they take fodder to the water-buffaloes but do not milk them; they look after the children. Fairly regularly, small, toddling infants stagger near the edge of an island and fall into the water. Then, all the women in the immediate neighbourhood shout and yell warnings in a deafeningly shrill hullabaloo, and the mother and her larger daughters rush to the rescue.

From the age of about six, the boys and girls are trusted to take their own small canoes out into the reeds like grown-ups; and they go for the day, cutting reeds or seeing that the buffaloes do not stray too far, singing in the undergrowth, and when older, no doubt, experimenting with sex. (The sex life of Marsh boys and girls is much the same as that of anyone else. It starts with a good deal of masturbation; continues with slap-and-tickle in the reeds – very discreet, this, because of the dire tribal penalites for 'going too far' – and culminates in early marriage, at about the age of twenty-three for a boy, and between fourteen and about eighteen for a girl. Apart from that, there is the occasional transvestite and effeminate dancing-boy. But the open eccentrics are rare.)

Traveller after traveller has commented on the beauty of the Marsh girls. They are as extraordinary as ever. Here they do not wear veils permanently stifling and hiding their beauty. But they are shy and diffident before strangers, turning quietly away and twitching a corner of their headcloths across mouth and nose. In the home, they are a powerful influence: they abandon reticence there. In times of war, the tribal women have always been the ones to rouse reluctant warriors to battle with blood-curdling ululations and blood-stirring war-cries. They are the ones who consult with other mothers in whispered cabal when a marriage is in the offing: is the girl suitable, chaste, responsible, a good cook? Is the boy healthy, a good worker or a slacker, a thief? These important matters are thrashed out by the mothers in conclave. The counsel of the older women is sought by the men, heard respectfully, and often acted upon. Women are not only considered to be good at producing heirs, warriors and workers, and providing the evening meal. They are a back-parlour power in the land of the Marshes.

The Marshes were not always bathed in sunshine. There were misty dawns, chill and ghostly grey as the beginning of the Sumerian world. Cold winds whined down the reed waterways no longer beautiful with tiny flowers, but dull and unfriendly. Sheets of rain hissed across the water. At this time, the giant lagoons seemed turned to lead. They were suddenly very dangerous. One moment you were in flat water with low ripples sipping at the gunwales; a minute later you could be rowing for dear life to the shore, with a raging wind throwing black waves into the *tarada*. Every year people are drowned on these lagoons, and sometimes whole wedding parties have been engulfed.

I was plunged one night into the icy fury of a full Marsh gale.

I had separated from Thesiger. With my usual canoe-men, I had been to Basra so that a doctor there could look at Chethir's throat. He complained of pain and I could see two or three nasty whitish spots deep in his gullet; though strong in arms and legs he looked delicate and I did not want to leave things to chance. After an injection or two he felt better and we rejoined our *tarada* where I had left it with Haji Hamaid, the master boat-builder of Huwair, where all the Marsh *mashhufs* are built. While we were with the Haji a messenger arrived from Awaidiya, the village of Jasim bin Faris, the sheikh of the Fartus. The Fartus grew rice and were Madan. 'Come at once', Jasim's message said. 'Nasaif's wedding is to be tomorrow.'

Thesiger had introduced me to Jasim; they were devoted friends. Jasim was extremely popular with his own people and respected throughout the Marshes. A tall, thin figure with a lined, kind face, he must then have been about sixty years old. I had stayed with him often, shooting duck or pig from his modest *mudhif*, which was very small and looked as if it would topple over sideways. It was always fun staying with Jasim; apart from the shooting there were singing and dancing parties in the evenings and games and stories and laughter. Jasim had been a great warrior. He had fought British soldiers and sheltered other Madan from them – Badr bin Rumaiyidh, 'the Old Man of the Marshes', hid with him for a year. He had two sons, Nasaif and Falih; the former slow and strong and hardworking, the latter more fun-loving and quixotic. Nasaif had told me he was soon to be married and he and his father urged me to be there.

When Jasim's message reached us we were delighted. We shook the Haji's hand without delay and Hafadh and Hasan briskly shoved the *tarada* off into the deep water. We had to get a move on; it was nearly sunset and Jasim lived far away. In the event the journey took a long time. We had only travelled for about an hour when the wild winds from the mountains of Kurdistan swept roaring down on us like an avalanche of icy air. In a trice the setting sun disappeared and blackness descended. Dark clouds streamed low over us. Unidentifiable birds flashed by like dead leaves snatched by the wind. We fled into the reeds for cover. The reed heads frothed and reeled and the wind screamed like a thousand devils through the reed stems, but at least we couldn't be swamped there. It was terribly cold. We wound the black and white headcloths over our noses and chins so only our eyes showed. I slipped my 7mm Mannlicher-Schönauer rifle into its canvas cover and my companions plugged the muzzles of their rifles and made sure their cloaks protected the cartridges in their cross-belts and the daggers at their waists from flying spray. They had to stop paddling from time to time to blow on their hands or thrust them under their arm-pits for warmth. The wind froze our spirits. It crushed the will to sing, even to talk.

After a while we came to a group of houses, miles from anywhere. 'My brother Sahain has a friend here,' Hafadh said, his lips to my ear. We shouted to the inhabitants for permission to land, yelling ourselves hoarse in the tearing wind. People came out and embraced Hafadh, and presently we took on board a low metal contraption, like a tray on four legs, full of hot coals. This brazier was placed amidships and we cast off again into the storm. Through the night we took it in turns to warm ourselves at it.

At long last the wind died, the clouds cleared and we saw sharp, cold stars. We still shivered but at least we could see ahead.

In the Marshes' heart, one soon learned that the lethal hazards of tribal life were not mere romantic pretence. Since we left Huwair the boys had kept their ears pricked for the slightest sound. Suppose we heard a thrashing noise from the reed-bed – 'pig,' Ajram whispered without breaking the stroke; perhaps a ripple in the water alongside – 'an otter,' Chethir would breathe in my ear. But if another sound came, the soft sound they instantly recognized as a paddle, our *tarada* was suddenly full of tension. Our paddling stopped, cloaks were pushed back to free the shoulders for action, two of the boys eased their rifles up (they were already loaded with one cartridge ready in the breech) and we drifted silently in the darkness, totally alert. Then Ajram would shout:

'*Yahu hai*? Who's that?'

And a deep-throated voice replied:

'*Sadiq*: friend.'

'From where?'

'People of Such-and-Such a tribe going to So-and-So. And you?'

'We are with the Englishman on our way to Jasim bin Faris's.'

'Ah, yes. Nasaif is to be married. You are with the Englishman – so Ajram is there. I greet your father Haji Hussein, Ajram.'

'God protect you!' Ajram called back.

Relieved, the boys laid down their rifles, took up their paddles again, and we moved on. The strangers could have been tribesmen in blood feud with the Feraigat – blood feuds were frequent. If so, we would have needed to get our shots in first to remain alive. *Fasl*, the paying of compensation for a murder in money, women, or buffaloes, was still the tradition. An *atwa*, a temporary truce between two feuding parties guaranteed by some respected man like Sayyid Sarwat, was still the common way of staving off open warfare or a rash of vengeance killings. But bloody scrimmages in the reeds were frequent. Added to this, armed bandits sometimes roamed the waterways. Like everybody else, my companions automatically followed the discipline of centuries and were constantly vigilant.

At Jasim's village, Awaidiya, white moonlight lay on the curved rooftops like a blanket of snow. After the gale, several of the smaller houses had a lurching, stricken look. When we reached Jasim's small, cock-eyed *mudhif* he welcomed us and, refusing tea, we threw ourselves down in our blankets and slept like the dead. With dawn, the wedding ritual began. The village was quick with life. The Fartus gathered excitedly round their sheikh. Men and women in *mashhufs* emerged from every lane in the reeds, chattering and grinning. All the men were got up to look their fiercest, their chests criss-crossed with bandoliers, rifles in their hands, daggers in their belts; the women in anklets, bracelets, head-decorations which tinkled and chinked as they moved. Jasim controlled everyone and everything, welcoming, organizing, his voice low and gentle, his tall, bowed figure at the hub of things, waving his battered cigarette-holder like a conductor's baton. When everyone was present, at Jasim's command we all embarked in a swirl of haste, and a long, jostling, rocking, convoy of boats wound off through the reeds to the village of Al Qabiba where Nasaif's wife-to-be waited with her family.

The celebrations at Al Qabiba continued through the day. The tribal standards were raised on a large *ishan* and the men began the *hosa*, the tribal war-dance that precedes marriage or battle. The tribesmen stamped and hopped rhythmically in a circle round the great flapping flags of green and black. They fired their rifles over their heads so that the air sang with bullets. Men snatched off their headcloths and waved them hysterically; and the women, their hair, shoulders and arms glinting with silver decorations, ululated shrilly in the background. Then, with the fever of the occasion still upon them, the entire tribe took to the boats again and with much shouting, singing and random firing, returned to Awaidiya.

I travelled in Jasim's *tarada* with old Jasim himself and Nasaif, his newly-wed son, who flushed and sweated with excitement and embarrassment. The young bride, a demure figure with a Mona Lisa smile and lowered eyelids, travelled in front of us with her father and a large *mashhuf* heaped with her possessions – brightly coloured mattresses, cushions, an old wooden bedstead, a chest of drawers with one foot missing. As we sped erratically along, Jasim, the veteran of several tribal wars and fights with the Turks and the British, called out 'Foq hum! Foq hum! Onto them! Onto them!' – the battle cry of a sheikh urging on his men in a charge – and the firing redoubled.

The night – momentus for the Fartus – was long, and for hours Jasim's small and overflowing *mudhif* roared with shouts and songs and laughter. A number of people were obliged to sit outside. Inside, in a minimum of space, several young men danced the sinuous, solo dances of the Madan to the throb and click of hand-drums. Jasim himself sat quietly puffing at his cigarette-holder, gently content, until Nasaif, according to custom, rose, scarlet in the face, excused himself and stumbled out of the *mudhif*. Followed by a cacophony of ribald comment, he was expected to go home, consummate the day's marriage and signal that happy achievement by firing a single shot from his house. In the *mudhif*, while we waited for him, desultory conversation continued in an atmosphere of anticipation. For a time the whole village hung in almost audible suspense. Then: ppranggg. . . ! And cries and song burst out again as Nasaif's single shot echoed across the Marsh.

'Is your shotgun loaded?' Jasim called to me through the hubbub. 'Let off a couple of barrels into the roof here.'

'But the holes will let in the rain.'

'Never mind. Let the rain come in. The holes will be a souvenir of Nasaif's marriage and your visit!' I put two barrels of number five shot into the roof to great applause. The holes were still there when I left the Marshes four years later.

Good times. And there were other times – so many that they are unaccountable – that were good without something special like a wedding to enhance them. I mean all the ordinary evenings spent sitting with my Arab companions in small *mudhifs* or smaller houses, sleepily listening to the unceasing conversations about local affairs – crops, prices, a recent murder, a newly hatched blood feud – or to hilarious stories and to the songs which, unlike much of the sad singing that charmed the reed-beds, were often robust, even jolly, and sometimes had choruses that everyone could join in.

At Al Qabab there was a particularly fine singer called Jahaish (little donkey). 'Yes, yes,' his enraptured audience cried between each verse. 'Beautiful. Give us more, more.'

'Do you sing, Hafadh?'

'Hafadh sounds like a frog. Don't ask him.'

'What about an English song?' someone would ask at last.

'Oh, I don't sing.'

'Don't the English sing then? Give us a song.'

'Sing, sing, sing!' – at least ten people would be shouting, the canoe-boys in the lead. There was no refusing them. So I croaked out 'Three Blind Mice', which one or two had already heard from Thesiger. It proved to be a great favourite. Sometimes in the months to come, on a distant lagoon you heard an Arab voice carolling 'Three blind mice, three blind mice, see how they run, see how they run. . . .' Only the passage about the farmer's wife was inclined to be badly garbled.

When we spent the evenings indoors, the low-burning dung-fires or the pressure lamps flung deep shadows like great mysterious wings across ceiling and walls, and the darkness enfolded us in a comforting cloak of intimacy. Bats, restless in the evening, flew up into the roof, hooked themselves there upside down and, hanging like wicked fruit, went to sleep. Thick coffee was ground and we sucked it up noisily drop by drop; tea was brewed and re-brewed. Outside you heard the wind and the dogs, the splash of a paddle, a shout of 'Who's that?' Round the fire the age-old Muslim oaths punctuated the talk like hiccups – 'By Abbas, I tell you, it is true' . . . 'By Hussein' . . . 'By God' . . . 'By your honour.' (Disaster, it is said, will surely overtake the man who breaks the great oath 'By Abbas' – the Abbas, that is, who is nicknamed '*Abu'l ras el harr*, the Hot-Headed One,' son of Ali, the Prophet's son-in-law and nephew, horribly killed at Kerbela.)

At length, one by one, people straggle off to their own homes. Those who are left roll their cloaks into pillows, spread out mattresses if there are any, and stretch out under a single blanket. If they have them, they draw their rifles in beside them, entwining an arm in the sling in case of thieves. The fire is damped down and the ashes scattered. A small hurdle is set across the door to keep out the buffaloes. The lamp is turned out. A few murmurs of sleepy conversation. Someone scratches an importunate flea. Then you hear the sharp, teasing whine of mosquitoes and it is time to wind your *kefiyah* round your head and cheeks and draw the blanket over your head. And sleep.

I was still working in the Basra shipping office. But I was going more and more to the Marshes. I was not skimping my office work but there was a great danger that soon I might begin to. My heart was with the Madan. I could think of nothing but them. So presently the fateful day that had to come finally came. I had joined up with Wilfred Thesiger for a spell, and we had spent an exciting time shooting pigs, sometimes from the canoes, at other times flushing them on foot from their shelters on the banks of the dykes. At the end of it, we returned to a village where the hospitality was outstanding – not grand, but lovingly offered; the best sort. That evening Thesiger and I sat idly gossiping on a bright orange rug stretched across the rush-strewn buffalo-platform of our host's small house. Our companions sprawled around us talking quietly to some visiting men of the village. It had been a very hot day. Now the breeze was a benison; but I was far from happy. I had to start back to Basra next morning. Hafadh and Ajram would go with me to buy medicine, new cloaks and a cartridge belt for Sahain, and then return. I was not sure when I would be able to visit the Marshes again.

Thesiger turned to me. 'Well, have you decided what to do? Are you going to try to be a director of a shipping firm in twenty-five years' time? Or will you resign, take your chance and stay here and then go to Arabia as you told me you wanted to?' He was right. The question had to be faced. Better to face it today.

The Marsh Arabs I knew so well by now looked across at us and grinned, not knowing what was being said. The two *taradas* gently rolled and nodded in the water alongside. Skeins of belated duck passed overhead. Though I had no money of my own to fall back on if I resigned from my job, only one decision was possible.

'Well,' said Thesiger, 'will you stay with the Arabs?'

I said, 'Yes.'

Our host came out of the house and, smiling, motioned us in to take coffee.

'Yes,' I repeated. 'Of course.'

Many months later, I faced Hafadh and Ajram and the rest in Sahain's house and wondered how to say goodbye. I was going to leave Iraq for a time to travel in the southern valleys of the Hejaz mountains. I could not stay forever, year in, year out, in the Marshes. But the farewells were not easy. It was a question of keeping misery under some sort of reasonable control.

'Goodbye, Sahain. I'll be back.'

'Soon, God willing. Don't forget us.' Sahain pumped my hand up and down between both of his. 'Don't you forget *me*,' I said. We stood on the rushes outside his front door. There was quite a crowd there.

'Will you look after this, Hafadh?' — I handed him the Mannlicher-Schönauer we had shot the pigs with, the bandolier and the remaining ammunition. This is for you.'

Hafadh was overjoyed. Tears ran down his face. 'If he doesn't look after it, I'll beat him,' Sahain said, smiling.

Then I left them. Presently the *tarada* dipped through the reeds towards Sayyid Sarwat's guest-house and on my way to Basra and the outside world. It was not a happy moment.

10 Wild Beasts, Cattle and Creeping Things

The bird and animal life of the Marshes combines with the lively, lusty Marsh Arabs themselves to ensure that the region is not a mere beautiful, stagnant backwater of the world. It lies on a major bird migration-route, and the birds and animals of the area add a thrilling dimension to the beauty of an already extraordinary landscape. Recently one particular animal from this region became world famous, and made its owner an international best-seller, so perhaps that small and humble mammal should take precedence here over grander beasts like the lions or wild bulls that the sporting kings of Assyria pursued about southern Iraq, or the huge wild boars which still infest it.

I met this unusual animal through a coincidence. In February, 1956, I returned to Basra for a short visit after two years wandering in south-western Arabia. The first day I decided to call at the British Consulate-General. There, to my surprise and delight, as I walked through the door of an ante-room, two Marsh Arabs who I recognized instantly as Ajram and Hasan bin Manati, sprang up and ran forward, grinning, to greet me. Behind them, a slim Englishman with long blond hair, wrestled intently with a struggling sack that seemed to have a life of its own. Presently he looked up, smiled, and said, 'Hullo. Please excuse me. My name's Gavin Maxwell. I see you know these two. They've just brought me this down from the Marshes. Stand clear a second. There's something very interesting in this bag and it's coming out.' Almost at once a very small otter emerged from the sack and peered about. Maxwell picked it up and began stroking it and talking to it soothingly while Ajram,

Hasan and I looked on. This baby otter, about six weeks old, flew with Maxwell to London next day. He christened it Mijbil and it soon achieved notoriety in his best-selling book, *Ring of Bright Water*, but only, alas, after its death at the hands of a Scottish roadworker.

Mijbil was Gavin Maxwell's second Marsh otter cub. The first – a female – was found by Wilfred Thesiger in the eastern Marshes and Maxwell paid five dinars for her (then worth about five pounds.) He called her Chahala after the tributary of the Tigris near which he first saw her. She had webbed feet, was about the size of a kitten or a squirrel and had a 'stiff-looking, tapering tail the length of a pencil'. But Chahala died quite soon of a sudden and mysterious fever she contracted in the Marshes and Maxwell, miserably, watched her tiny corpse float away in water carpeted with white and golden flowers. So Mijbil came to take her place, and his darker fur and flatter tail proclaimed him, Maxwell said, 'a very important otter' – in fact, as it turned out, of a species new to science (Chahala had been a 'conventional', European otter). And when Mijbil had been examined by the zoologists in London, he assumed a new official, scientific name: *Lutrogale perspicillata maxwelli*. Otters of the Maxwell and European kind still abound in the Marshes. They are particularly common round the lagoons, such as Zikri, Dima or Barkat Baghdad, where they breed in February and March. Marsh Arabs spear them if they can and sell their skins in the towns.

Lions roamed the edge of the Marshes until relatively recently, though whether the last lions were shot during the First World War or not long before it is not clear. Sumerian relief carvings show, in brilliant detail, lions attacking cattle, or heroes, including the great Gilgamesh, grappling with them. The Assyrian kings seem to have been pathologically opposed to all lionkind. They organized large-scale lion hunts and lavishly decorated the halls of Nineveh with sculptures depicting lions at bay and transfixed by royal arrows. The Assyrian ruler, Ashurbanipal (668–627 BC), who went after them relentlessly on horse or foot, pronounced the lions of the Marshes to be so

numerous as to constitute a pest. By his time killing them had
assumed some religious significance since Ashur, Nergal, Nin-
urta and Ishtar were all patron gods of lion hunting.

Henry Layard (later to become Sir Henry Layard, the first
excavator of Nineveh and Nimrud), the man who had commented on the beauty of the Marsh maidens and the reed
architecture of southern Mesopotamia in 1843, also reported
that the local inhabitants engaged in 'regular lion hunts on the
banks of reed- and bush-lined streams'. One day, resting with
some Arabs travelling from Hawaiza to the Shatt al Arab near
the great swamp full of high reeds and salt water, he was
suddenly aroused by the firing of guns and by loud cries. 'I
jumped up,' he wrote in his diary, 'thinking we had been
attacked by marauders; but I soon perceived a large lion trotting
slowly away. He had been disturbed in his lair by the people of
the caravan searching for better water. . . . The shots fired
fortunately did not take effect, for had he been wounded he
might have turned upon us and done no little mischief. As it
was, he disappeared and we saw no more of him.'

Layard remarks of the lions of Khuzistan and Mesopotamia
that they are formidable animals, capable of carrying off a

full-sized buffalo; a bold claim. He adds: 'Buffaloes are said to beat (a lion) off by placing themselves back to back, and meeting their assailants with their bulky foreheads and knotted horns'. He describes a lioness (or was it a lion?) shot with a matchlock as measuring 10½ feet in length, its body tawny and light yellow, its mane dark yellow and black. And lions were not only to be found on the bank of the Shatt al Arab and the Tigris. Travelling north from Zubair near the Hor al Hammar, Layard says that to his Arab companions 'every bush appeared to be a lion'. Lions continued to haunt the bushes for many years. One or two aged retainers of Thesiger's friend, Sheikh Falih bin Majid of the Albu Mohammed, told us in the 1950s that they remembered hearing the deep, guttural roar and heavy grunting cough of lions carrying across at night from the Amara area. But, in 1976, when I asked the venerable Sayyid Sarwat, who grew up at Qalat Salih and whose age – though a trifle uncertain – must be the far side of eighty, if he, too, heard those roars, he replied, 'No, I've never heard any myself. But my father often talked of seeing and hearing lions hereabouts.'

The almost landless Marshes themselves are not, of course, an attractive prospect for many animals. But wolves still roam the dry Beni Lam country north of Amara; Thesiger saw several. Honey-badgers, too, are occasionally seen there and so are wild cats and hyaenas. Ajram swears that hyaenas of a striped variety attack sleeping children and even adults as near to urbanization as Mejar. And Amara tells of a hyaena that tore a man's face away while he slept, and relishes the final gruesome detail: 'the corpse could only be identified by its clothes.'

Leaving aside domestic animals like water-buffaloes, cattle and dogs, by far the most common animals in the Marshes themselves are the wild pigs. These are so prevalent as to represent a veritable scourge. They are enormous beasts, as big as donkeys, measuring 3 or 4 feet at the shoulder, and weighing 300 pounds and more. The British traveller called John Jackson found some just north of Qurna in 1797 and was amazed, as well he might have been. 'The country here is very little in-habited, being wet, swampy and covered with reed and willows.

I fired at a crane among the willows; and instantly, a large herd
of wild hogs rushed out, some of them of such size that at first
sight I could scarcely believe they were hogs. Their colour is
deep red.'

Wild pigs are as numerous as rats in a farmyard. Related to
the European and Indian boars but much bigger, they have
infested the Marshes from the beginning of recorded time.
Sumerian carvings show men hunting pigs with spears, a dangerous undertaking considering the immense weight and power
of these creatures, and their habit of turning and charging. A
hunter, armed only with spears, would be at a terrifying dis-
advantage in any encounter with an aggressive pig. Without a
high velocity rifle or heavy shot a man would be very lucky
indeed to avoid being knocked down. He would then either be
rolled on and savagely bitten (by a sow) or (if it were a boar)
ripped up the belly by slashing razor-sharp tusks.

Boars have charged *mashhufs* in shallow water, shattering
the wooden sides and hurling their occupants overboard. They
do most damage among Marshmen and cultivators who stum-
ble on them when they are lying up in reeds or high corn. Sows
are particularly dangerous in the spring when they sprawl in
their nests suckling their young. Apparently immobile with
lethargy and their own weight, they can spring up with horrific
agility and literally fall on an intruder in furious defence of their
piglets.

Layard wrote in his journals of Arabs driving wild pigs and
shooting them with matchlock guns along dykes and among
the tamarisk bushes and scrub. These days, far from dying out,
they are more numerous than ever because the Marshmen
cannot afford the expense of cartridges to shoot them. To have
some idea of the havoc the pigs can inflict on rice, barley or
wheat crops, one only has to envisage the sight of, say, forty or
even sixty great black, shaggy-haired animals, grazing together
in a rice field like so many monstrous sheep. With such a vision
in mind, one can understand the despair of the Marsh Arabs
who own the rice. Fired by this despair, young men will leap
onto backs of pigs they have surprised swimming in deep water

and drown them with clubs or by holding their hindlegs together with their bare hands.

All over the Marshes men display the scars of encounters with pigs. The shaggy brutes are something of an obsession. Whenever I have been out shooting them, local excitement has erupted in frenzied and voluble activity: every man and boy who can be spared from work springs shouting into a boat of some description and, armed with whatever he has been able to lay hands on – possibly a rifle, an old shotgun, a fishing-spear, or perhaps only a dagger – paddles excitedly to the fray. Apart from their satisfaction at the destruction of one of their greatest natural enemies, Marsh Arabs love the excitement of a chase and a pig hunt invariably brings out a large, chattering and milling audience. Occasionally a pig runs berserk amongst the spectators and someone may be savaged.

The image of these loathsome creatures does not fade. I see them now: enormous hulks galloping through walls of spray in water 3 feet deep; the dark silhouettes of boars 40 yards away swiftly raising their snouts and then wheeling head-on to charge; the obscene weight of a sprawling sow suddenly revealed at one's very feet in high reeds, the split-second terror at the sight of her, the end of terror as pig and gunsight spring up simultaneously and the high velocity, soft-nosed bullets smother her point-blank charge just in time. Pig shooting could be horrific, exciting, and very messy, and sometimes all three things at once. I started by using a gun Wilfred Thesiger lent me, a ·275 high velocity rifle made by John Rigby of London, perhaps the best sporting rifle of its calibre in the world. Later I bought my own gun, a lesser beauty but it worked well enough for me – an 8 mm Mannlicher-Schönauer. It was rather stubby, more a carbine than a rifle, with the wood of the stock continued up to the end of the barrel. The Marsh Arabs, who like giving everything a name, called Thesiger's Rigby *Rigeibi* – an affectionate version of the English name – but they had no hope of pronouncing Mannlicher-Schönaeur so they called mine *al Nemsawi*, the Austrian.

Marsh Arabs would use any means to shoot pigs. The damage

they did justified any means of exterminating them. If possible the Marshmen liked to catch the pigs in deep water where a canoe could be deftly paddled alongside the swimming animal and a bullet planted at close quarters through the back of its head. (It was not so easy if the pig, though swimming, turned and tried to upset the *mashhuf*.)

My first encounter with a pig was a small nightmare. I was in a canoe with Ajram and Hafadh when we flushed three medium-sized pigs from a clump of reeds in shallow water. I had never fired at a pig before. I selected one now, aimed behind its shoulder as it shot away at top speed and squeezed the trigger. The shot struck low and late, a heavy, expanding lump of lead ripping across its belly exposing its innards. It did not kill the animal; it did not even stop it. To my horror, the pig disappeared squealing miserably into the reeds, presumably to die in agony an hour or two later. After that, I took very good care when and how I fired at pigs; and that wretched perform-ance, thank God, was never repeated. Pigs were regarded as dangerous vermin and had to be reduced, no doubt of that. The Marshmen chided me for turning my head away when they set about spearing to death piglets they had found in an abandoned nest – the Massacre of the Innocents, I called it. 'Do you want them to grow up and kill us?' they demanded, quite irritably. No, one did not. But still. . . .

The most frightening way of shooting wild pigs, it seemed to me, was walking them up in dense reeds. It was bad enough walking them up on dry land, in the small clumps of date-palms and bushy undergrowth you find where the Marsh frays out into meandering channels through cultivation or pasture. The pigs creep into these small oases, curl up in the shade of a large bush and sleep. You can be on top of them before you see them. In the next two seconds – not more – they are either on top of *you* or making off hell-for-leather into the distance.

I preferred to advance into these pig-fortresses in a fixed formation: myself holding the Mannlicher, Hafadh, Hasan bin Manati, or one of the others who, I knew, could shoot reason-ably well, slightly behind me and to my right holding a two-barrelled shotgun loaded with buckshot. Sometimes someone else would be nearby with a fishing spear or a dagger, but one could not rely much on him. Once a very large pig shot out of a bush, tail up and head and tusks down, straight towards me at a distance of about 30 feet. There was no possibility of a reasonable shot; mine smacked into the ground well over the pig's head, and I braced myself for the bone-crunching impact of 350 pounds of pig somewhere around my waist. I had heard, as if from a very long way off, Hafadh's shrill cry of 'Look out!' – advice I hardly needed. By a miracle the pig swerved to my right and passed between Hafadh and myself like a cannonball. He brushed my legs. I felt the wind of him and smelt his meaty, muddy smell as the furry mountain – bunched muscle, hair, sickle-sharp tusks – shot by. The pig plunged into thick undergrowth. Hafadh's barrel of buckshot went for nothing among the branches, and he and I gazed at each other, getting our breath back.

Another time, Hasan, in unorthodox fashion, dropped to one knee as a pig was coming across him towards me and stopped it stone dead with both barrels of the shotgun fired almost simultaneously. This may give the impression that killing pigs was easy – simply a question of hitting them correctly. But it was more than that. You could hit a fast-moving pig square and it would still come on. I was far too timid to go after pigs with nothing but a shotgun.

Marsh Arabs are courageous in a crisis. One day Thesiger and his canoe-men were charged by not one, but two, exceptionally big boars as the canoe lay alongside the dry land. They seemed, with their heads lowered and their great shoulders hunched, about to hurl themselves furiously into the boat. It took five shots from Thesiger – each one audibly a direct hit – to stop them. When they finally dropped in a flurry of mud and blood at his feet, Thesiger turned to find his companions half-crouched, their daggers in their hands. He asked them what they would have done if a pig had got into the boat. Amara replied, 'We were going to jump on it and kill it with our daggers.'

Probably even more numerous, and as much prized as the wild pigs are hated, the water-buffaloes still lumber their way across the morasses and flatlands of southern Iraq like repetitive shapes on an old frieze.

At Sahain's house late one night, I went out into the buffalo-platform to relieve myself and heard a low voice at the unlit door of an island-house fifty yards away across the silent water. It was too dark to see; the house was a black hump in the water. Somebody seemed to be singing, but in a strange, jerky, strangulated way – and it was too late at night for people to be singing to one another. Next morning I asked about this unusual sound and people told me that it had been Ajram out on the platform under the stars crooning to a sick buffalo to comfort it. Ajram arrived later to confirm this. It was the normal thing to do, he said, although in this case the unfortunate animal had not recovered from its undiagnoseable complaint and had died just before dawn. 'What words did you sing to it, Ajram?' I asked. 'Oh, just words that came into my head,' he said.

Some houses have buffalo-shelters called *sitras* on the same island but separated from the house. But usually the buffaloes sleep outside the front door. Occasionally the calves are allowed into the house itself, with young cows, and you can be woken up in the middle of the night by a snort in your ear from a damp, inquisitive muzzle or by a bump from the hoof of a restless buffalo. No one ever seems to be seriously trampled in his sleep, I don't know why.

Buffaloes grumpily enjoy their wonderfully pampered lives. Every morning early the women have to chivy these hulks of fat, bone, horn and hide to their feet, before they can be induced to go off, loudly protesting the unpardonable intrusion on their privacy, to spend an utterly carefree day luxuriating in the lush grazing grounds of the Marsh. The scolding women might be suburban wives forcing recalcitrant husbands out of the house to face the day in a hated office: the buffaloes have to be swiped with rushes and sticks, shouted at and cursed before they move, in a reverberation of groans, to the platform's edge. There, in. what seems like slow motion, they splosh heavily into the water, setting up a small tidal wave that may cause a small boy passing in a tiny canoe to rock wildly and cry in alarm.

All day these lords of indolence wallow in cooling water and rich acres of edible sedges (called *hashish*). No man or beast will molest them. They can range safely and at will. They swim easily in deep water, or lunge their way through the reed-beds, incidentally creating new watery lanes that the tribesmen soon begin to use. They pant and gasp and stare blankly at the world with only their glistening muzzles and long-lashed eyes above water. I have seen buffaloes submerged so totally that only two black and quivering nostrils broke the water's surface. When they are standing on dry land, egrets and even small children can stand and sit on their backs but the buffaloes pay no attention.

In winter, the water is often too cold for them and they remain all day on their platforms, emitting their groaning, rasping, gargling sounds of complaint, and fodder cut by the family during a hard day in the reeds is brought and laid before their disdainful noses as if it was roast peacock before princes. Even in summer the family – every man, woman, boy or girl – sallies out daily to cut *hashish* which is presented to buffaloes that have already enjoyed a full day's free grazing in the reeds. The yearly outpouring of gallons of milk and curds and butter, and tons of dung fuel is well worth the family's efforts.

The value Marsh Arabs place on these buffaloes can be seen from the following prices I noted in 1976: female buffalo (in calf) 117 dinars; old male buffalo 76 dinars; one buffalo calf 35 dinars (1 dinar = £1.50).

The settled Madan families own between three and eight buffaloes. But the Madan nomads of the eastern Marshes move great herds from west of the Tigris to the Persian frontier. They used to have a surly reputation; in the old days constant stealing of buffaloes caused violent feuds and bloodshed among the tribes. Even so, the sight of these ponderous, black buffalo shapes is somehow comforting. What harmless animals they are after all; and how useful. Despite their bulk, they are hopelessly vulnerable and humanly neurotic. They pick up foot-and-mouth disease from the wild pigs; and drop their calves into the water; and they easily go out of condition if something upsets them. They deserve the devoted attention they get, because, despite their Walt Disney look, these creatures are the mainstay of the Madan way of life. They are at peace with all nature.

There is little I need say of other animals found in the Marshes – domestic cows, for example, or cats, or sheep, which manage to survive on the Marshmen's soggy island platforms. Marsh dogs, however, are worth mentioning because of their extreme aggression and because of the deafening dog-choruses that, day and night, shatter the peace of villages: a distant shot, a sudden shout, the appearance of a *mashhuf* carrying one or more strangers on the edge of the village, sometimes no more than a buffalo's strangled bellow at the back of the house, can act as the switch that starts off a mad cacophony of frenzied barking. High-pitched yelps, gruff, choking roars, full-throated howls without any apparent pause for breath, blend into a maddening bombardment of sound that can make you lie under your blanket praying for silence to return. It seems an age before the dogs turn, growling, back to sleep, and you are left to the soothing rustle of wind in the reeds and the cronk-crunk of the frogs.

Marsh dogs not only bark, they are savage biters, too. They will go for strangers as if to kill and only someone they know can bring them to heel. Other Eastern countries have their guard-dog populations, and it is as well to watch out for them if you are approaching a village in, say, Thailand or India. But the village dogs of southern Iraq are a ferocious breed apart. I think they are bigger than other people's. They look much thicker and stronger round the neck and shoulders, although not much taller, than Indian pi-dogs. They fight furiously amongst themselves, sometimes four or five together in a terrifying *mêlée* of teeth and gurgling roars. Most have battered, pugilists' heads and often an ear or an eye missing. They are used to being hit with stones or sticks by members of the household they guard (it is often difficult to restrain them any other way). I would never try to stroke a Marsh dog, however docile it looked or however near to it and me its master was sitting.

Once, walking from Sayyid Sarwat's house to a village not very far away and on dry land, I was surrounded by a large pack of frenzied dogs – I would say about twelve or fifteen – that charged in on me like a swarm of maddened bees on the attack. By the grace of God, two men from the village were walking towards me not very far away. They began running towards me and shouting at the dogs, which I was having the greatest difficulty holding off by hurling stones and lumps of earth. I can see now the uncurbed fury in those dogs' eyes and the fangs that chopped the air closer and closer.

One of the largest dogs raced towards me with such determination to tear me apart that it was unable to stop and smacked into me in a cloud of dust. A canine head as hard as oak thumped my calf. Luckily the shock of the impact alarmed the dog as much as it did me and it cringed away before rejoining the attacks on me from a distance. The two villagers beat them off. But these dogs could kill.

The man would be extremely unlucky who found himself within striking distance of two other dangerous inhabitants of the Marsh area: sharks, which are very rare visitors; or snakes, which are common but prefer to evade rather than attack man. Sharks have been sighted in the Basra roadstead – so I was told when I lived there – and, according to local gossip, they occasionally attacked bathers in the Shatt al Arab. People also talk of sharks spotted at rare intervals in the Tigris as far up as Baghdad. But the story one of his colleagues spun to General Chesney of a 15 foot long shark in the Euphrates near Qurna seemed pretty unlikely to him. 'Shark?' he huffed sceptically. 'A whale more likely.' I heard Marsh Arabs now and again insist that they had seen small sharks in the Marshes, and this is possible at flood time. Be that as it may, you are unlikely to see one.

Snakes abound, especially in the summer. One should keep a good lookout for them. The bite of a certain species, called *arbid*, is fatal. As we were travelling in the *tarada* one hot day near Dima Lake, the prow-man, Jabbar, suddenly called out, 'Look, an *arbid*. On that island. Let's get it.' I thought he had seen a snake in the reeds and wanted to leap ashore to tackle it. But a foraging Marsh Arab had got there first and killed it with his spear. Jabbar held the snake up on the end of his paddle: an ugly-looking thing, about 4 feet long with an underbelly of ivory-white.

Sometimes these Marsh snakes wrap their coils round reed stems and hang there in the sun. That 4-footer was a mere tiddler compared to the mighty serpents that do move about the reed forests. Reddish monsters, several feet long and as thick as a man's forearm, slither through the sodden undergrowth and no wonder the Marsh Arabs fear them: they are things you hope won't crop up in your dreams. In former times, Marsh Arabs invented a mythical snake-monster with supernatural properties which they called *Afa* or *Anfish*. Today, they simply keep their eyes open and avoid stepping on the unmyth-ical *arbid*, which I imagine is a kind of viper.

I have left the birds to the end: they are the Marshes' crowning beauty. From November to early spring, the lagoons and reed-beds are flecked with the flashing colours of halcyon kingfishers and the gaudy purple gallinule, and the sky is dotted with floating eagles or mottled with whirling concourses of geese from Siberia and wild duck of many kinds. Summer is not the time for birds. After spring, most of them have gone. The long, sinister-looking cormorants fly low across the water. There are still scores of herons about, too; both the tall, round-shouldered Goliath heron – almost man-sized – and its smaller replica, the pigmy heron, inhabit the marshes year in, year out. Marsh Arab folklore of long ago has it that herons slept in flocks, one bird being chosen to stand sentry. Forbidden to sleep, he balances on one leg, supporting the other foot against his knee, so that if he does begin to doze he will immediately topple over. Woe betide a heron 'sentry' who does so sleep and topple: the other herons peck him to death. Or so the Madan used to say.

Winter is the time of porcelain-blue skies and countless birds. You see most kinds of duck: pintail, widgeon, teal, mallard, shoveller, red-crested pochard, gargany, diving duck, and white and black tufted duck. There are white ibises, too, and hoopoes, red hawks, avocets, stilts; warblers of all kinds perching on reed stems, unafraid, or twittering unseen; and black and white kingfishers, bee-eaters, yellow-billed storks, African darters. Eagles always seem to be drifting overhead and white-tailed sea-eagles, quite tame, breed in the reed-beds. A large predatory bird the Marsh Arabs call a *haum*, which is either a harrier or an eagle of sorts and has wide, dark, canopy-like wings with an impressive span to them, skims the top of the reed-beds, looking for coot and moorhen. Finding any in open water, the *haum* dives onto them with a surprisingly abrupt contortion of wings and body. Tribesmen out shooting coot and not having any luck point eagerly to a hunting *haum* and paddle towards it for dear life knowing that coot are there.

The lagoons are often dark with thousands of blue-black coot. The eagles dive and dive on them trying to panic them into individual flight; they like to take these plump, eatable birds in the air. But, although coot have a sheep-like air of stupidity, they are wise to an eagle's tricks. When the eagle's dive-bombing begins, they huddle even closer, then spread their wings and skitter across the surface, beating up a dense cloud of spray which is usually enough to decide the eagle to go hunting somewhere else.

Marsh Arabs often urged me to shoot one of the most common birds in the Marshes, the pelican: and I as often refused to do so. Pelicans are harmless and look far too dignified and far too vulnerable: firing into them would be like mortaring a congregation of bishops. In any case, pelican meat is inedible, and the tribesmen simply want them for their stretchable neck pouches which the Madan say make the most resonant skins for their hand-drums. Ungainly they may be, but pelicans at rest, their pure white feathers and yellow bills reflected in the mirror surface of a lagoon, ride the waters with ship-like grace. They can be beautiful. Standing in the shallows to feed, at evening, several hundred together, they stoop and pluck and preen, making a sea of agitated whiteness that slowly turns to flamingo-pink as the sun sinks. And high up, slowly wheeling and wheeling on outstretched, unmoving wings, these some-times ludicrous-looking birds give to the sweep of water, reeds and towering sky an extra touch of majesty.

But above all other creatures, the geese and duck lodge in the memory. Their wild sky-armies come whirling and crying out of the Russian tundras and seem to carry with them much of the spirit of the Marshes. When the duck seethe on the skyline in dark, shifting clouds like smoke or bees or locusts: as the descending grey-lag or white-front swirl across an evening sky that is pearl-grey and flecked with tongues of flame-coloured cloud: when darkness has fallen and the village noises have died away and the sad goose-calls come from the grazing-fields, it is time to be silent and let the wild creatures have the Marshes to themselves.

11 Return to the Marshes

I went to the Marshes first, as I have described, in early 1952; and I returned to them numerous times and for much longer periods after I had left Ralli Brothers. Then I left Iraq for two years of uninterrupted travel in the south-western Highlands of Saudi Arabia, from the sand and mountains of Taif, Bisha, Najran and the Asir, to the humid saltflats of Lith and Gizan on the Tihama coast. In 1956, I flew back to Basra on my way home for a holiday in London and was reunited for a short happy time with the Madan.

My life with Marsh Arabs had made it easier meanwhile to adapt to the ways of the sterner, tribal *bedu* and hill-peoples of Arabia. Naturally the terrain I lived in in Arabia – dusty and arid to the east, superb mountains with running streams and orchards to the west, the tawny plains of the Red Sea coast – was about as unlike the marshlands of Iraq as anything could be. The Arabic dialects were different, too. I look back at those months in Arabia as some of the best in my life. But the Marsh Arabs were the people I had met first – and that, in terms of affection, makes a subtle but essential difference.

As it happened, almost as soon as I arrived in London for that short holiday in 1956, the Suez crisis erupted like a political Vesuvius. Overnight, Britons became outcasts in the Middle East and it was quite impossible to return to the area as a traveller. I had left baggage and books there. I had left Arab friends behind with farewells still unsaid, and no way to write to them because they could not read or write and, besides, had no fixed address. To make going back still more impossible, a revolution in Baghdad ended the monarchy in Iraq, and plunged the country into a decade of political turbulence. So many years went by before I could even seriously think of returning to the Marshes. I became a foreign correspondent for *The Observer*, saw a considerable part of the rest of the world, witnessed a good many wars and upheavals and became deeply attached to other places and other peoples. Despite this, the dream of that return never left me.

Now and again sensible friends advised me to forget the Marsh Arabs. 'Never go back,' they said. Perhaps it is good advice most of the time. You are certainly asking for disappointment if you go back to a once-loved place after as much as seventeen years. Memory of a first love seldom fades. The danger is that time can twist memories into strange, false shapes.

All the same, when in 1973 an official in Baghdad said to me, 'Yes, of course, you can see the Marshes again,' I didn't hesitate. It was only later, in the car on the road south from Baghdad to Amara, that I began to worry. I knew there had been changes. Sheikhs (or most of them) had been dispossessed; water had been controlled, possibly reducing the area of the Marsh; land had been distributed to tribesmen. But the nearer my Chevrolet taxi came to the Marshes the more I began to imagine other, more drastic changes. Suppose the Marshes had been largely drained? Suppose the people I knew had migrated untraceably to jobs in Baghdad or Kuwait? Suppose they were dead? I actually suggested stopping and turning back to Baghdad, but the driver looked at me as if I were mad. And it would have been a shabby retreat.

After we had crossed the Tigris at Amara, landscape and sky flattened out exactly as I had remembered. The car bumped to a halt on the water's edge more or less where I had found Thesiger beside the *tarada* twenty-one years before. This was a chilling moment. For now, in a few minutes, I would know what had happened to my Marsh Arab friends and whether it was worth while going on. The information would come from a tiny police post which lay just ahead on the waterway I was staring at – a Beau Geste fort with a complement of, perhaps, a sergeant and four men. Beyond that post there was nothing but Marsh. The policemen's 'beat', at least in theory, extended south from the fort into the Marsh. The policemen, therefore, were the people who would tell me the best or the worst.

I left the driver with the car and walked to the little white-washed fort. As I approached, a policeman came out to meet me. He was fat, fifty-ish and his chins were covered with a greying stubble. He wore a khaki uniform jacket over a *dishdasha*, the ankle-length Iraqi shirt. He looked at me curiously. And I stared tremulously back at the chins and stubble of this man who was about to announce the future.

'Good evening,' I said.

'Good evening.' He shook my hand. He was looking at me fixedly. 'Odd. Haven't I seen you before?'

'Well it would have been twenty years ago.'

'Yes, it was many years ago. And you came with another foreigner. You used to go into the Marshes.'

Thank heavens I had not forgotten all my Iraqi Arabic. 'That's right,' I said. This was the moment of truth, and not a moment I enjoyed. 'What happened, do you know, to all my friends? I mean Sahain, and Amara, and Hafadh, Sahain's brother?'

'You mean at Al Qabab?' He took an age lighting a cigarette from a red and white packet with an old lighter that sparked with difficulty.

'Yes, there and other places.'

'Oh,' he said, slowly blowing out smoke. 'They are here. Sahain, yes. Amara, you'll find him. Perhaps Hafadh is dead. I'm not sure. . . .' I swung away.

'Is there a boat?' My haste startled the fat policeman – he did not know that I felt like embracing him for the news he had given me.

'There's that launch,' he said doubtfully, pointing at a decrepit motorboat with a wooden roof that lay on the water. A man in a dirty *dishdasha* and a small boy, covered with oil and holding a spanner, crouched over its engine-housing, repairing something. 'How much to Rufaiya?' I said to the man. He looked up.

'I am not going to Rufaiya again until morning,' he said. It was true that the sun was lying very low on the horizon. It would be dark in an hour and a half at most.

'Look,' I said. 'This is urgent. I must be there tonight. Whatever the fare, I'll pay three times more.'

'Three times? All right. Bring your baggage.' He thought a second longer. 'Wait. I shall have to come back without passengers and in the dark.'

'Four times the fare,' I yelled at him, and he said, 'Get in.' The oily boy ran to the stern-rope and cast off. With a couple of quick twists of the starting-handle, the motor spluttered into life and the boat edged away from the bank. 'Salute Amara for me. Tell him I'm coming to see him soon,' the fat policeman called. 'I will,' I called back. 'I owe you a thousand thanks.'

'What for?' he shrugged, turning slowly back into the fort, where a transistor radio was giving out some football results from Baghdad.

You cannot hurry the owner of an ancient motorboat whatever you do. The engine stopped twice in mid-stream while the man and his boy-assistant unhurriedly hammered metal deep in its bowels, and these halts were not good for my patience. But slowly and surely we meandered down the winding Wadiya channel that I remembered so well. The water ran as swiftly and as muddily as ever. The pied kingfishers dropped into the water from their diving-boards in the willow trees as they always had, and the small mud-coloured turtles slipped down as usual into their mud-holes in the nick of time as our wash swept towards them. The same stubble of grass covered the low banks on either side. The same angry, orange sun was slowly quenched in a mauve evening haze.

There were some visible changes. On the skyline behind us I saw a towering meccano-like structure. 'That's the new sugar factory,' the launchman said when he saw me looking at it. Later – 'The Sheikhs used to live there,' he said, when we passed the fork in the channel where Thesiger and I had disembarked at Falih's *mudhif* – an empty place now where clouds of midges danced in the evening light. 'Yes,' I said, 'I remember.'

It was dusk when we came abreast of a big *mudhif*. 'Sayyid Sarwat still there?' I asked. He was, the launchman said; but I wanted to push on to Amara's that first night. We passed a fine-looking *tarada* moored to one of the Sayyid's willows and a lot of barking from the Sayyid's guard-dogs, and presently turned right into the Rufaiya channel. By then, the light had gone. We slid into Rufaiya, squeezing between the narrow banks; the dark avenue of trees loomed like a menacing smudge. I saw again the long huddle of arch-backed reed and mat houses that lined both sides of the channel between fields of barley stubble and rice. The boatman slowed the engine, reducing our wash. The small glimmer of lighted doorways grew larger. The first dogs rushed out at us. Dark figures moved on the bank in the blue-grey haze of evening fires. Rufaiya! 'To Amara's house,' I said.

Amara had been Thesiger's beloved companion. I retained a vision from all those years ago in Basra of a small, slim figure smiling gravely up at me when Thesiger introduced us, and then just as gravely offering me a handful of Huntley and Palmer's ginger biscuits from a silver box on the British Consul's tea-table. After that, in obscure parts of the Marsh, I had met him whenever I met Thesiger. They had parted for ever at Basra Airport in 1958. I had not seen Amara since 1956.

'Amara's house,' said the boatman uninterestedly. We bumped the bank and the boy skipped ashore with the mooring-rope, and people standing there in the darkness beat away the snarling dogs. There were voices saying *'Salaam aleikum.* Peace.' A rough hand grasped mine and helped me to the land, and the boatman handed up my bag. Several people greeted me, but no one I recognized. And then I saw Amara. His face was suddenly illuminated by a leap of flame from an open fire (it was warm weather and they had been sitting round their tea out-of-doors). It was a long, lined, rather worn face, with a day's stubble and a neat black moustache. He was now taller and, like me, a good deal older. I knew him at once from his eyes; deep-set, rather sad, or, at least, resigned-looking eyes. But I knew that he had not recognized me, despite his murmur and handshake of welcome. At that moment he was turning away to see to the tea for us.

'Amara,' I called in English, 'Amara, you bloody boy, damn and blast it!' It was the only English Amara had ever known. It had been Thesiger's shout of protest in the stress of doctoring if Amara dropped the syringe or handed him the wrong medicine-bottle. It had soon become a joke-phrase to all our Marsh friends. When Amara heard it now, he stood stock still with his back to me. Then he wheeled round, eyes wide, and an expression of astonishment and gladness that I shall never forget.

'Sahib!' He came back to me in two strides, swiftly grabbing my hands. 'Oh, it's a long time, a long time,' he said.

'Twenty years, Amara. Bloody boy. You had forgotten.'

'No, no! I couldn't see you in the dark. I have never forgotten.' He led me to sit down on the rugs that lay round the fire. Now things were quite different. Excitement filled the atmosphere like electricity. The crowd and confusion increased. A man shouted, 'Make coffee. Bring the cushions.' There was a sound of dogs being angrily thumped; people calling from more distant houses; the splash of canoe-paddles in the water-channel. I sat bemused in the centre of a human whirlwind, hardly able to grasp where I was, while Amara continually seized my arm and cried, 'How are you? How is Thesiger? Where is he?' And among the crowd Hasan bin Muhaisin's beaming face appeared and he shouted the same questions. 'How did you get here?' and 'Where did you come from?'

The boatman and his lad were surrounded by questioning people, and the boatman explained at length how he had found me and brought me, and how I had refused to wait until next morning, and how I had refused to stop at Sayyid Sarwat's on the way, and how he, the boatman, had nobly agreed to bring me despite the lateness of the hour and the darkness, and how now he must be on his way because he was exhausted and his boy . . . and well, yes, he would have a cup of tea, God give you a long life.

A lot of people came that evening, from Rufaiya, and from other villages on the edge of the Marsh proper. We sat and drank tea and coffee and then more tea. I could see Amara's intent, wondering eyes fixed upon me. He brought his small children to shake my hand and carefully explained to each one who I was and who Thesiger was and where we had travelled together. 'Is Thesiger really in Africa?' he said. 'God is wonderful!' And, laughing: 'You don't look *very* old. No older than me at least.'

Later he conferred loudly and with much gesticulation with Hasan and his two neighbours, Farhan and Idan, the sons of Saghair. 'Tomorrow,' he said, coming back to me excitedly, 'tomorrow we shall borrow Sayyid Sarwat's *tarada* – it's a fine one – and we'll go into the Marsh. It will be like the old times. Do you remember Sahain? We'll go to Al Qabab and see him and have a lovely time.'

Nothing could have been better than this. We talked and talked, and at last the crowd thinned away. It had been a long day. I pulled up the blankets Amara had given me and lay down. I stared at the swarm of stars overhead. I felt the warm breeze off the nearby, unseen Marshes and the old belief returned that I could smell the water of the lagoons. I felt the amazing *space*, the unchanged, open land and waterscape spreading, it seemed, limitlessly away around me. I heard Amara's deep, gentle voice still murmuring to his friends a little distance away. The seventeen years of my exile slid away, as if I had been able to flick back the meter of my age and become a scrawny youth once more with a job of shipping in Basra. It had been right to come back.

Presently, Amara left his friends and came and tucked in my blankets. Then he squatted down cross-legged beside me as if preparing for a vigil. Hasan and Farhan joined him. They gathered their cloaks round them comfortably and opened their tobacco boxes and began to roll cigarettes. 'Go to sleep,' Amara whispered, 'I am going to sit by you for a while. After all, this is your home as well as mine.'

12 The Marshes Today

Early next morning Amara said, 'The *tarada* is ready. Shall we go?' Sayyid Sarwat's war-canoe lay there – the one I had dimly seen moored to the channel-bank the night before. It was long and slender and its prow swept up sweetly: a thoroughbred beauty. 'There's one condition,' Amara said. 'The Sayyid insists you call on him when we get back from Sahain's. But he says keep the *tarada* as long as you like.'

The *tarada* was a godsend. I soon discovered that the great canoes had become very hard to come by. Since the sheikhs – or most of them – are no more, practically no one can afford to have a *tarada* built at Huwair. Sayyid Sarwat can still afford to, but these days he keeps his boat for others. He is well into his eighties and too old and bulky for rocking about in *taradas*.

The way to Al Qabab had not changed. I sat in the *tarada*, my tin box of medicines and films and a twin-flapped camel-saddlebag I had bought years before in the Hejaz behind me, and watched the familiar palisade of reeds close around us as I had the first time with Thesiger. Amara sat cross-legged amidships. He told me he had not been well; some trouble – a hernia perhaps – had forced him to avoid any strenuous work; he had never been strong, even in the old days. Farhan and Idan took up paddles in the bows; Jabbar, a powerful young man with a moustache and a face like a bedouin, crouched in the stern with a chunky neighbour of Amara's called Musa. Between them, they made the canoe sing through the water.

The morning was breezy with pale blue sky overhead and restless little clouds. The soft, creamy plumes of the reeds dipped and danced. The warblers flicked about in their jungle of sedge and eagles lazed about the sky. We burst out into Dima Lake: the soft, blue mirror of the water and the white, heaving blanket of pelicans seemed not to have moved since I had last been there.

Farhan sang: Amara talked – 'Yes, Rufaiya's grown. Well, we have more land now. Since the sheikhs it's been distributed and we all own what we farm. My son goes to school at Umm al Hosh. They have a 150 boys there and six teachers.' I had not seen Amara's friend Sabaiti the night before. 'He's a merchant in Mejar el Kebir now. We must go and see him. He's grown quite fat and has a lot of children.'

The familiar tinkle of water trailing off the paddles; the sudden flap of great awkward wings as a startled heron took to the air; the unmistakable, unique phrases of Marsh Arab talk: how could I have feared that the sounds of the Marshes would have changed?

'I had better tell you,' said Amara. 'Sahain is still headman here. Hafadh, Sahain's young brother, is dead; he suddenly fell ill. And Yasin is dead, too. He was shot. Some sort of blood feud, I think.' Poor, big, gruff, quarrelsome Yasin, I thought. 'His sons and wife are living in Al Qabab.' And soon we were there. The curved mat roofs appeared above the reeds.

'Behold Al Qabab!' shouted Farhan, and the rowers put on a new turn of speed to enter another tribe's village in style.

Al Qabab. In the old days it had always been a home from home for me. It has grown – today it has well over a 100 houses. Bu Mugheifat, where Sahain used to live, was abandoned years ago and the people, all of the Feraigat, concentrated round Sahain, like a swarm round the queen-bee, in Al Qabab.

Sahain was standing at his door with a paddle in his hand. There was no mistaking him. His face was more deeply lined and his hair was grey, that was all – the same strong, short body, eyes wrinkled with laughter and the glare of sun on the water. There was no doubt about his welcome either. The effect of our arrival in Al Qabab was more tumultuous even than at Rufaiya. Ajram soon arrived jubilant and grinning – unchanged as far as I could see but with a canoe-load of sons and brothers. Sahain's sons, Bani, Mohammed and Warid, the eldest, just back from military service, darted about preparing a sumptuous meal: sherbert, wheat bread, dishes of green beans, apricots, chicken, thick and spicy soups, yoghurt, a plate of lamb stew, grilled fish. Others piled onto Sahain's buffalo-platform which began to sink and seep water so that people ran to fetch bundles of rushes to raise the floor-level.

Middle-aged men demanded to be recognized, and I realized that these weather-beaten, lined faces belonged to the smooth-skinned, naked young swimmers of those scorching summers years ago. Among them was Chethir, no longer the delicate, slender figure of the 1950s, but a furrow-faced man of about thirty-six with dark, thick forearms and chin-stubble that scraped my cheek when he greeted me, and a hand that squeezed mine painfully. His hands were like paddle-heads and the pores on their backs were enormous. I knew him instantly, as I had Amara, by the deep eyes that the years had left unchanged. 'How's your throat, Chethir?' I said: I could see in my mind's eye those ugly, white spots that I had had treated by the doctor in Basra. 'Do you remember that?' he said. 'Oh, it's fine. Not a day's trouble with it for years.'

Sahain said: 'You know Hafadh's dead. He was your friend, wasn't he? There was nothing we could do. He had some pain in his stomach and chest. The doctor was baffled. And without warning one day, he just collapsed and died.' Sahain's eyes glistened. 'I already miss him,' I said. 'So do we,' said Sahain. 'Did you know he blew off half his hand with that gun you gave him? Yes. Some idiot got a bullet jammed in the barrel and Hafadh, not knowing, loaded and fired another bullet and a piece blew out of the chamber taking his thumb away. Look.' He went behind the mat partition in his house and came back with the Mannlicher I had left with Hafadh in 1956. Sure enough the chamber had been breached and repaired. I had never heard of an accident like that before. I was glad it was not the gun that had killed Hafadh.

'Sit down,' said Sahain smiling and taking my arm. 'Sit here and tell us what you have been doing.' He shouted, 'Hurry up with the tea, Ajram, make some coffee will you. Warid, my son, throw over more cushions. You two sons of Yasin, come over here and let Gavin look at you. You remember Yasin?'

'Very well,' I said. And to the boys, who quickly squatted close to me with folded legs and wide brown expectant eyes – about ten or twelve years old and with the Mongol cheek-bones of Yasin – I said, 'I have some photographs of your father in my bag. I'll show you later. He was very strong, and brave with pigs, and very dear to us all. Ajram will tell you I speak the truth.'

Ajram grunted, 'Yes, that's God's truth.'

The pattern of the old days began to re-form. We went shooting coot and duck for food. Then I deserted the *tarada* for a tiny 4-foot skiff – a *chalabiya* – which was essential in the narrow, overgrown reed-paths, half-lost except to Marsh Arab eyes and Marsh Arab memories.

I preferred an elderly man called Safair as my guide: an expert hunter even by Marsh standards; a skinny, undemonstrative man with a long nose like a snipe's; a brilliant tracker despite the extraordinary old-fashioned, round-framed glasses he perched on his nose. Safair shot skilfully with an ancient, single-barrelled shot-gun, sometimes concealing his lanky frame for hours in a reed-clump to wait for duck, like an old and bespectacled heron watching for frogs.

In the deep grey-green womb of the reeds I felt the old comfort. It pleased me to think that we might emerge from the Marshes to find Ancient Sumer around us; that in Basra there might be a Wali and Janissaries lounging in the bazaar, and Portuguese galleons in the Shatt al Arab; or that the Caliph Ali sat plump and white-bearded in his capital at Kufa with its new clay and reed mosque, and that Baghdad was still an insignificant village on the Tigris waiting for Harun al Rashid to build his city there.

There was a school at Al Qabab now. A large *ishan* covered with reeds and rushes, and three reed schoolrooms, and a small reed house for the two schoolmasters, cheerful young men on a nine-month secondment from a town near Baghdad. All the village boys went to school each morning. I saw them paddling themselves there or being paddled by their mothers. They sat at tiny desks in their *dishdashas* – all the sons of people I had known since they were the size and age of these children, when the idea of a school would have amazed them. In the summer, mosquitoes permitting, lessons are in the open air. 'Look now,' says the teacher at the blackboard. 'This is a three. What is it?'

'Three, three!' the class yells in unison and a couple of cattle egrets on the roof flap away in alarm.

'One, two, three,' says the teacher.

'One, two, three!'

I see Ajram weighing some fish on the platform of a house next door. He waves. His sons, Battel and Khanjar (which means Dagger), are in the class. In the evening Khanjar sits beside me at Sahan's to practise his English on me: 'How old are you? What is my name? One, two, three!'

At a larger village some hours away, I saw a school prize-giving ceremony, and a handball game in which the star was an enormously tall black boy, a sort of Harlem Globetrotter of the Marshes. He told me he was twelve years old, and he must have been at least 6 feet tall.

The village was visibly more prosperous without having changed too drastically. People's clothes looked much less ragged. Launch-owners, like the man who had taken me to reach Rufaiya, ran a more or less regular shuttle service to the markets. The launches move at a sedate pace and their roofs give one a grandstand view of the passing scene. The engines of some may smoke and splutter. But generally their quiet chugging hardly ruffles the peace of the Marshes, and their size confines them to the deepest channels, so you do not meet them head-on every bend in the reeds.

One early trip I made in the *tarada* was to Jasim bin Faris's far out at Awaidiya. I had heard that the wonderful old man was still miraculously alive. Jasim was one example of a sheikh who had been so beloved by his people that they had voted for him to remain over them. I looked forward to seeing his stooped, deceptively languid figure with the cigarette-holder, and see his little smile and hear him encouraging the festivities, as he had at his son Nasaif's wedding, with '*Fog hum!* Onto them!' the old battlecry. But Jasim was away in Shatra, not at all well, said Nasaif, who welcomed us. Jasim's younger son, Falih, who soon arrived from Shatra, confirmed it. The old lopsided *mudhif* had gone and with it the two holes I had shot into the roof a few minutes after Nasaif's consummation of his marriage. A bigger, grander structure stood in its place. In fact, prosperity had come to the Fartus. Nasaif was now head of a new cooperative organization, set up within the tribe, for marketing fish. *Bellams* brought ice – I had scarcely seen ice in the Marshes before – and the fish were shipped in it to Basra or Amara. Tribesmen came as I watched and emptied fish from their skiffs onto an already impressive pile. Nasaif would pack the fish presently into a *bellam* full of ice for the market and later divide the sale-money to all concerned. 'Hard work,' Nasaif said, 'with the crops and buffaloes, too. But worth it.' Certainly: Marsh tribesmen now earn two or three thousand dinars a year. An enormous sum in Iraq. His and Falih's hospitality was as lavish as ever. Falih took me out to the places where at that winter-time of year the geese came in to graze.

Only the Berbera had netted and sold fish in the old days. Now everyone in the Marshes is doing it, including Ajram.

'You've all become Berbera now,' I told him.

'With a family like mine, I have to earn money somehow,' Ajram grinned. Then added: 'Do you remember my first son's birthday party?'

'I remember Mister Kharaibat very well.'

'Well, there's Kharaibat the second now. And Battel, and Alwan, and Khanjar and Ali!'

'Isn't it time to stop?' I said.

A grin and a shrug!

On one shooting afternoon, a party of us went to Bu Mugheifat – or where Bu Mugheifat had once been. The water completely covered it. I looked into the water and saw the

ishans deep down and drowned for ever. 'That's our house!'
Sahain said, pointing. And other people shouted, laughing,
'That's mine' . . . 'And that's mine!' But it was disturbing to see
the past imprisoned down there.

Sahain's house today is a good deal larger than his old one.
It is snugly built of reed columns and reed mats, with an earth
strip for a coffee hearth near the low, Alice in Wonderland
door. I thanked God that the evening's entertainment did not
centre round the deafening, idiot sound of a transistor radio.
There is the familiar sprightly hubbub of humans talking to
humans, and jokes, and songs. On the warm evenings rugs are
spread outside. We sit watching the swallows dipping down to
drink in flight and listen to the frogs' chorus and the groaning
of the buffaloes and the noise of the birds in the reeds – the
sunset air is always full of little voices. Now and again you hear
in the distance – sounds carry in the reeds – the long stutter of
a modern sub-machine gun; and another stutter, or perhaps
several, replying. Sahain and the others will prick up their ears
and say, 'That must be a Such-and-Such a place.' It means a
blood feud is being fought out. And, indeed, Sahain's people
themselves were in blood feud because a ne'er-do-well of the
Feraigat had eloped with someone's daughter in another district. Sahain had a good deal of trouble before a truce could be
arranged and guaranteed by Sayyid Sarwat. The girl's relatives
were furiously demanding *fasl* – compensation. Otherwise, they
snapped and barked – 'Your people, Sahain, should henceforth
guard their lives well, whether cutting reeds or hunting or
merely travelling to market, they should be careful!' – that was
the warning. The compensation they were demanding was two
girls of marriageable age, plus about £700 in Iraq money – a
lot of money in the Marshes. When Sahain had asked for a
period of truce in which to find the kidnapper and return the
girl, he had been rudely rebuffed. So he sought help from Sayyid
Sarwat. With that incomparable assistance and the backing of
the local police-chief (who is wisely content to leave tribal
problems to the tribes unless things really get out of hand), a
truce was arranged for six months. It had later been renewed

for a further period. But Al Qabab had some uneasy nights and days before the truce. I noticed people were quicker to call out '*Yahu hai?*' at some suspicious night-sound. And the response '*Sadiq!* Friend!' came quicker, too.

The British administrators after 1915 found that a harsh code of honour governed the Marsh tribes. Haji Rikkan told Hedgcock of a young man who, on hearing of his sister's adultery with a neighbour, went straight home and stabbed her to death, saying, 'Sister, the price of adultery is death'. Surely he acted a shade too brusquely? No; it was agreed by all that the brother had been right. No one would have risked making a false accusation of adultery for which the punishment is dire. So the taleteller had not been lying; and the brother was obliged to kill.

The lore of the Marshes is very old and it is not simple. The varying compensations (*fasl*) that can cancel blood feuds have to be learned like a more complex multiplication table. Women or buffaloes can make up the price, as well as money. But how many of one and how much of the other depends on who has killed whom; what relationship, if any, existed between them; what tribes are involved, and so on. The passions and vengefulness of a volatile and heavily armed people to whom honour is paramount and who live far from the constraints of government must be effectively curbed or channelled somehow.

In the old days everyone had a bolt-action rifle and was proud of it. Now smuggled automatic weapons are the thing. Ammunition is hard to get and expensive, but this does not stop people loosing off hundreds of rounds for a wedding or funeral as tribal custom demands.

When Haji Yunis, the grand old man of Al Aggar, a good friend of Thesiger and myself, died in 1976 at a great age, it was said that three or four thousand rounds were banged off into the blue in his honour – although perhaps nobody really counted. One of the Haji's last acts had been to present Al Aggar – a big, sprawling village, almost three villages in one – with a winnowing machine. It was a great, old-fashioned thing of enormous, clanking wheels and snapping belts and had been built some years ago by a firm called Ruston of Lincoln in England. It snorted like twenty dragons, and took several men tugging on a rope to get it going. Haji Yunis encouraged them with shouts of 'For the Love of God, heave!' as they strained at the rope that turned the great driving-wheel. 'Heave! Heave! God give you strength.' Several score villagers danced and clapped encouragement and at last a heavy metallic cough shook the machine; a dense cloud of oily smoke enveloped all concerned; then it was away and grinding. It was old and noisy but, thanks to God, it worked. Haji Yunis was much blessed for the innovation.

At the village of Saigal there are now two or three communal mills like Haji Yunis's at Al Aggar. Saigal stands on the lip of the marsh and is the most populated place in the west-central Marshes. There must be a thousand families living there, some on dry land and some on islands.

There is a police fort, too, that turns orange-red when the setting sun strikes its old bricks. What is more, there is a small concrete clinic with a young Iraqi doctor called Fuad and a nurse or two. The doctor's clinic was always full when I visited it, with a queue of patients squatting outside the door, fanning the flies away from sores and cuts. I had never seen a doctor in the Marshes before. People came to Fuad from a long way around. He has a small white launch as well as his clinic and he chugs about the neighbouring villages two or three times a week, bandaging and inoculating, rather as we used to, but I suppose with a more comprehensive knowledge of surgery. In the last few years I have come across him in several villages, once near Jasim bin Faris's at Awaidiya. A cheerful man, he told me that bilharzia is much reduced – though it is a vigorous disease that stubbornly resists elimination: all those hostsnails must be annihilated with their lurking parasites. But TB is the main trouble now, and trachoma and dysentery and bronchitis. Malnutrition? No, says Doctor Fuad; and I did not see or hear of any. There are other doctors at, I believe, Sahain (a biggish place north of Saigal), Shatanya (even further north), Shatra, Chubaish (a major township on the Euphrates) and Mejar el Kebir, and people with some degree of medical training at several other places on the northern edge of the Marshes, like Negara and Humus.

Of course, the extra cultivable land given to the Madan after 1968 had improved their diet and I saw many fewer infant stomachs swollen by vitamin deficiency. Each peasant *fellah* has received from the Government five *donums* (a *donum* is an area a little less than an acre) and some Marsh tribesmen something like seven or eight *donums* of good land supposing there was enough in the reasonably close vicinity.

'Only in the belly of the Marsh', Amara told me, 'are there people who still rely on nothing but fish, buffaloes and reeds for their livelihood.' As for the Feraigat, they received more like three to five *donums* each. To reach the Feraigat barley and rice fields takes about three hours by canoe from Sahain's

house; but that is nothing to a Marsh Arab. At the necessary
season of the year they go out at dawn and back at sunset, or
after, bawling out songs at the top of their voices and thinking
nothing of it. It is revealing – how strong and proud tribal
feeling is – that the Marsh Arabs are not deserting their Marshes
for the already overstuffed cities as many *fellahin* are. The
slower-minded *fellahin* began their pursuit of gold in the streets
of Baghdad and Basra in the mid-1950s. They are in hot and
usually futile pursuit of it still, having apparently learned
nothing all these years. Not the Madan. Why? Chethir's answer
was short and simple: 'In the water, the reeds and the air, is
where we live and where we like to live.' And that, for him, was
that.

'Sayyid Sarwat says take the *tarada* as long as you like. But on
one condition. You must visit him as soon as you can.' Amara
had told me that first morning of my return. It was no hardship
to visit that saintly man of stormy good-nature. The crew of
the *tarada* always enjoyed staying with him. They, like people
from the farthest extremity of the Marshes and beyond, hastened to consult him on topics ranging from unlawful arrest or
adultery to sheep-rustling.

'Well, well, well!' he rumbled when we tied up alongside the
mudhif, the new concrete guest-room, and the tiny outside
lavatory on the water's edge. 'How was the *tarada*? Watertight?
Not a bad one, is it? Wouldn't give you something that was
falling apart! Now then, how long is it since I saw you last?
Was it with Thesiger? – Yes, that's right, just before the sheikhs
went away. How are you, Amara? Look after my friend here,
eh? Mind you do, and God help you!' He threw out his arms,
looking enormous in his wide black robes. 'Do we have to stand
all day in this heat? Have all the rugs been stolen? Has someone
sold them all? Why don't you bring some so our friends can sit
down? Jabbar, how are you – family well? I heard they cut out
your mother's gall-stones. Well, God preserve her anyway.
Come now, Gavin, sit by me. I see my family has left me one

rug unsold, thank God. . . .' This is the ebullient, unstoppable way the Sayyid addresses his guests and those around him. He is eighty-something by now, he tells me, though even approximate ages in the Marsh region are elusive.

He dyes his beard black and chuckles about it like a boy. His rain-barrel body and his deep-chested boom of a voice are undiminished. He alarmed his family and friends in 1975 by flying off to Baghdad to have a serious eye operation: he had become almost totally blind. The excursion became a triumph. The hospital was quickly infiltrated by swarms of visitors demanding to see the Sayyid. The doctors had prescribed post-operational calm, but the invasion force was irresistible and the Sayyid asked for and was instantly granted a special room for callers, and meals – at the Sayyid's expense, of course – were specially prepared for all comers. Luckily the operation was a success; Sayyid Sarwat can now see well enough to read the huge illuminated Koran which the Government has presented to him.

For the last few years I have gone straight to his house each time I visited the Marshes. 'Welcome, welcome', his mighty voice reverberates round the willow trees at the water's edge, bouncing roundly off the amber-coloured walls of his reed *mudhif*. 'Bring cushions. Where's the tea, where's the coffee? Hurry up! Hurry up! My friend is waiting and you stand about doing nothing.'

In fact, people are already scurrying about in all directions – giggling happily, taking the Sayyid's mock anger in fun. Most of the dark, surcoated, running figures, some rather too plump for all this darting about to bring jugs of sherbert or trays of tea, are the Sayyid's sons of whom he has eleven or twelve, or at least a great many. The oldest must be in their forties or fifties by now.

The youngest, Sayyid Abbas (the title *Sayyid* is inherited), goes to school in Baghdad and is a good-looking boy of about seventeen, bright and perfectly mannered. When we meet in Baghdad, Abbas will sip a glass of beer (of course, in theory his religion and status reject alcohol) saying mildly, 'One must experience everything in life, or how does one know about it?' I cannot imagine Abbas performing a malicious act. Goodness shines out of him like a light from a lighthouse. It is a sign of the time that he wants to become an engineer. Also that one of his brothers, Mottar, works today in the sugar factory at Mejar that I had seen from the launch on my first day back.

Between Sayyid Sarwat's house and the factory stretches a green, undulating ocean of sugar. 'It's full of wild pigs and black partridge,' Mottar says excitedly. 'Let's go and shoot some.' And so we sometimes do, he still wearing the blue factory overalls. He showed me over the factory once, proudly and expertly – it's a big, complex set-up but Mottar knows it all. Other workers called out to him in a friendly way as we went round; he is obviously popular there – and not just because he is a *sayyid*. Unlike the Marsh Arabs, the socialist-inclined industrial workers of the Amara area are no respecters of religious titles. They like him because, like his father, he is a good man.

Sayyid Sarwat and all his family do southern Iraq honour with their sanctity. The Sayyid himself personifies all that is irreplaceably fine in Iraq, in the Arabs and in Islam. His house is a sort of unregistered place of pilgrimage. I have seen senior Iraqi officials consulting him – once I met a judge from Amara city, and once the Governor of the Province himself dropped in. One day Sayyid Sarwat interceded for Amara – he pays avuncular attention to small, ordinary people. Amara had, through some misunderstanding, failed to pay a fine to the local court and was suddenly in danger of a short but most inconvenient imprisonment. The Sayyid had a muttered word with a visiting town counsellor from Mejar over tea and sherbert. The official came over to me before leaving to say, smiling, 'Don't worry about your friend – what's his name? – yes, Amara. It'll be all right. The Sayyid says he has known him since he was a boy. He says he's a good man.'

When one of his sons – a favourite son – was killed in a motor-cycle accident a year or two ago, people commiserated with Sayyid Sarwat. The old man brushed them aside gently, saying, 'It was written.' When he himself dies, there will be a funeral to surpass all funerals. His *cortège* to Nejef will be famous.

Sayyid Sarwat's *mudhif* has a few interesting details attached to its history. It is big, but certainly not the biggest in the area. Still, he told me that when it was constructed in 1957, men came from villages near and far to lend a hand. It took four months to fix the eleven great reed wall-pillars in the ground, another month for the vertical pillars at the ends, and another six days to arch the pillars together and bind them. Twenty-seven sheep it took, he said, to sustain the workmen, and on top of that the cost of rice, bread, sugar, gallons of tea and coffee and hot lime-tea and sherbert and yoghurt for as many as two hundred men a day. Perhaps it cost £3000 or more. You sit on reed mats on the floor in this sublime guesthouse, which I think is the best way, because it is comfortable and because if you put tables and chairs in a *mudhif* you destroy the symmetry of it. The Sayyid has a superb set of coffee-pots on his hearth ranked like chessmen, and they and the walls and ceiling of the *mudhif*, where the bats lurk, are stained black with the smoke of years. Dusty electrical fixtures hang from the roof. Luckily they do not work – the mellowness of oil lamps is appropriate here. The Sayyid's modern four-pillared plaster and cement guest-house is better suited for electricity and it has wooden benches and light metal chairs to sit on, too. It was built for officials who think the old Arab way of sitting cross-legged is uncomfortable or undignified. In the warm weather, the Sayyid's servants and sons set out metal folding-chairs and we sit watching the herons stalking about like hunched, feathered skeletons across the waterway, and listen to the black partridge calling.

At such times I ask him about old tribal customs; he is an unmatchable authority. The swearing on the flag of Abbas, for example, colourfully described in Hedgcock's book *Haji Rik-kan*, was one ritual I thought might have been forgotten by now. Its purpose was to end a blood feud. Warring headmen would gather to take an oath of peace on behalf of their people, and their manner of doing so would be more or less as follows: 'Bring a reed as long as a man. Lay it on the ground crying – "This is the sword of Abbas, of Abul Ras al Harr!" Take a white *dishdasha*. Lay it by the reed, cry: "This is the flag of Allah, of Mohammed his Prophet and of Ali, and its avenger is Abbas. This flag is for me, on my eyes and on my life, on my brothers and on my kindred. Nothing is concealed nor hidden, and its avenger is Abbas". Tie a corner of the *dishdasha* round the reed. Then, the other participants tie a knot saying, "I tie this flag on me, on my brothers and on my kindred!" ' To a tribesman this oath is no light matter. I wondered if it is still the most solemn oath in the Marshes, and if the ritual is the same as it was in 1919? 'Certainly it is,' the Sayyid boomed. 'Wonderful that you should have read that in an Englishman's book. Of course, there used to be a lot of English about. A channel near here is called El Grimliya after an Englishman, Mr Grimley. I think he was the Consul in Amara.'

A year or two ago, I arrived at this heart-warming place to find the Sayyid, arms spread, crying, 'Take a look at the *tarada* – your *tarada*, I mean. Just look at it.' He had had it painted white from stem to stern, and sky-blue inside. I only had seen the classic black *taradas* up to then; I was not sure that I liked the white. But it grew on me – and on Farhan and Idan and Jabbar and Musa. We grew proud of its difference. In the reeds it looked like a white ghost, and, gliding into a village with all eyes upon us, like a proud white swan.

On one of many excursions in the Marshes since my return there in 1973, I re-visited Huwair to see if boat-building was a vanishing art. Sayyid Sarwat had told me that the old master boat-builder, Haji Hamaid, had retired. His honourable place had been taken by Haji Abdul Mehsin, who had built the *tarada* for Sayyid Sarwat. We found the Haji and his workmen busy on several canoes at once in a backwater of Huwair among palm trees and small canals. A stack of nearly finished canoes filled one of the Haji's larger sheds. The Haji said, yes, there were more launches in the Marshes nowadays. 'But our trade still does well,' he added. 'Do you know we turn out 200 *mashhufs* every month? Some big, some small. Size varies according to demand. On an average we charge fifteen dinars (about thirty-five pounds) and a good one should survive five years' heavy wear-and-tear.' What about the Rolls-Royces of the canoe-world, the *taradas*? 'I see you have the *tarada* I built for Sayyid Sarwat,' he said, slapping her prow. 'A good one, that, even if I say so. Well, since the big sheikhs departed, not many people can afford a *tarada* any more. It would cost you nearly £200 now. That is, if I can get enough of those big-headed nails to line the inside planks with. But let me know when you want one – I'll make you one, don't worry.' And this good-natured man, who daily performs a carpentering skill almost as old as the world itself, gave himself ten minutes off to drink tea with us.

The Marshes have their eccentrics, of course, like everywhere else. There is the man at Al Aggar who regularly disrupts the guest-house by arranging, when it is late at night and dark inside and the *mudhif* is full (and most of the older, local men have paddled off to bed), for most of the lights to be doused. He then crawls in on all fours, his face a mask of ghostly white powder, his nostrils forced to twice their size by two reed twigs in his teeth and his eyes rolled up until they are almost invisible. He groans horribly. 'The King of the Marsh! The King of the Marsh!' the younger ones scream in mock hysteria, and, I suspect, with a touch of real terror. The *mudhif* is suddenly an uproar of people fleeing in fits of laughter from the advancing 'phantom'. In olden times, Marsh people were fervent believers in this 'King of the Marsh', whom many claimed to have seen – a gigantic negro, according to some; a great shining-faced, roaring shadow blotting out the stars, said others. Today people deny they believe in such things, just as in Europe and America most people reject the idea of ghosts and yet would avoid spending the night alone in a reputedly haunted house.

Shibil, the seventeen-year-old son of Chethir, has an interesting quirk of character. He has his father's high cheek-bones, green eyes and a nature that is half wistful and half quicksilver. He also has the same curious, touching habit that his father had at his age. When I used to take Chethir to the doctor in Basra for treatment of those sinister white spots in his throat, he would emerge from the clinic quite silent and apparently sunk in thought. Soon, when we were sitting somewhere away from the crowded street, he would turn to face me and, still without a word, begin very gently and with great concentration to trace with his forefinger the contours of my face. 'What is it, Chethir?' I might say – in the circumstances it was difficult to remain totally silent. He would smile very faintly and say absolutely nothing. The silent finger moved on. In a moment or two he was back to normal, laughing and chattering once more, telling me what the doctor had said to him, asking what we would do tomorrow and so on. Shibil sometimes does the same now, though this has no connection with seeing doctors. His finger lightly and slowly passes across my eyes, down the line of the chin, caresses the jaw, follows the (deepening) lines from nose to mouth, and all the time there is this expression of total absorption on his face. The green eyes say nothing and neither does he. It happens in idle moments when two or three of us are lolling around gossiping. It is curious; it embarrasses no Marsh Arab who happens to be there; and there is no explanation. Most of the time Shibil is to be seen splashing and shouting in high spirits. Everyone says he, like his father, is a good hunter and fisherman.

In 1976 I asked officials in Baghdad if they could arrange for me to see what the Marshes looked like from an eagle's point of view. I had seen it, of course, from the Iraqi Airways flight from Baghdad to Basra, but from that height you see too many clouds. Presently, I was lent a helicopter by the government; two days to tour the Marshes from the air. 'Let it come to my house!' Sayyid Sarwat said at once when he heard. I passed on his invitation to the pilot, an Air Force officer with a large moustache, and a genial manner, and he accepted.

The helicopter had made a considerable sensation by clattering down immediately outside Sayyid Sarwat's *mudhif*, its rotor-blades barely missing the outside brick-built privy. People came running excitedly from neighbouring villages. The Sayyid, of course, had ordered a feast to be prepared for the pilot and his crew.

'Anywhere special you want to look at?' the pilot shouted. I tried to direct him to Al Qabab, but it was much harder to find than I had imagined. From above, the little hump-backed houses were scattered far and wide, all looking the same. We dipped and circled until our fuel ran low. At last, thank heavens, I saw it. The pilot let the machine fall sharply and we flew in lowering circles over the school and Sahain's house and the other *ishans*. The buffaloes leaped into the water in panic. But men and women ran out of the houses waving, and back and forth over them we flew, waving back. After five minutes we made one last low 'run' over the village and then whirred back to Sayyid Sarwat's.

Next day we travelled to Al Qabab in the *tarada*, a three hours' haul. When everyone was packed into Sahain's house that night round the fire, I said: 'Did anyone see an aeroplane over here yesterday?' There was an immediate outcry – 'Yes, yes, of course! We saw you in it! Why didn't you land here?' I said: 'How can you have known it was me up there? We were too far up for you to see.' (I hadn't been to the Marshes for several months and I was not expected.) Chethir said, 'Who else would it be? Of course it was you.' Ajram added: 'We hoped you'd land.' 'But where, Ajram? The school-island is too soggy. Your buffalo-platforms are far too narrow.' But they repeated, 'We had hoped you would land.'

Never go back? Who can say 'never'? There are good things to be reminded of.

I had forgotten the quality of inwardness of the unveiled Marsh women which replaces the rosy richness of the flesh of their extreme youth, and which is no less attractive. It is good to remember how the Marsh Arabs have names for everything they live beside. Ask an Indian or a Malay 'What do you call that bird?' and he says 'Bird'; you ask 'Please, what is the name of that flower?' – and he replies 'Flower'. But a Marsh boy knows the brilliant little kingfisher is called 'the sheikh's daughter' and nothing else; he knows a Goliath heron as *zurgi*, and that the pigmy heron has its own name, *rikhaiwi*. He knows the ox-tongue plant, and the goose-flower, and the white and gold buttercup; he knows that *jat* is a gay, pink flower, not just a buffalo's favourite food. Marsh Arabs are lovers of life. Their zestful bodies and spirits might be delicately wired to the mood of the places they inhabit: to a joyful lagoon or a mournful one; to the wind thrumming happily through the reeds or howling menacingly over solid, black waves. It is good to hear across the reeds an old, old song of love – or even 'Three Blind Mice'.

Let me add that there is a vision in the Marshes that all men might see with profit and take away. I mean the towering dimensions of the sky: the sky's hugeness dwarfs everything. And nothing so much as the figure of a man with a spear balancing a canoe on a sheet of water that seems to stretch to the edge of the world.

A Blessing

Changes have come, even to the seemingly unchanging Marshes. As I was writing this book, old Jasim bin Faris – I have described his elder son's wedding – died at Awaidiya. I have never met a finer man than Jasim: he had fought the British, then made friends with them, and he had shown Thesiger and myself what nobility there is in simple Arabs. A few months later in London, my telephone rang and I heard a voice saying in Arabic, 'This is Falih bin Jasim.'

'Who?' I said. The name did not seem to mean anything to me. Then I suddenly realized it was old Jasim's second son. 'Falih! What are you doing in London?' I knew he had hardly travelled as far as Baghdad before, and he speaks no English whatever.

'I have something wrong with me,' he said. 'I thought I would come here to see a doctor. Can you come and see me?'

I sped in a taxi to a small hotel off the Bayswater Road, and there of all places, I met Falih again, a small, nut-brown figure in a suit – the first suit of his life – with a neon sign over both our heads saying 'Lounge Bar' and a television set belching out something about a British athletics contest.

'Weren't you nervous, coming here all alone?'

'No,' he said, 'I thought I would find you, and then you would tell me of a good doctor.' He brought out a huge packet of dates and handed them to me – 'These are for you,' he said, 'all the way from Qurna! Shall we drink tea?' Despite the bustle of German and Arab tourists around us, we might almost have been sitting together, as of old, in his father's cock-eyed *mudhif* surrounded by reeds and water. His tribesmen contributed to the expense of his air fare and hospital bills. He was determined to have sons; the operation concerned fertility. The tribesmen agreed that that was worth paying for.

Twenty years ago, no Marsh Arab would have dreamed of visiting London. Of course, the rich landowners like Majid al Khalifah travelled abroad. But Falih is very much a people's sheikh. He and Nasaif, his brother, live and work with their people.

I asked Falih when he left hospital what he would like to see in London. He replied, 'London is a city like any other. What I would really like to see is your countryside, your peasants, and your water-buffaloes and cattle.' So we went to my old home in the depths of South Wales; he was amazed by the greenness of the rolling, rich arable land. One day, farmer friends took him to see a sheepdog trial involving twelve expert dogs and several score sheep. He was thrilled by all this, full of admiration for the farmers who, like himself, rolled up their sleeves and worked their own land and with their own animals. At one point his heart was so full that he burst into a traditional Marsh Arab song, and for a few moments the soft South Welsh hillsides echoed to a strange sound from a distant and quite different land. My gum-booted farmer friends listened fascinated, grins on their faces; but, I think, they were moved by his happiness. When Falih said goodbye to them, he astonished them by clasping them firmly in his arms and planting grateful kisses on their ruddy, yeoman cheeks. On another occasion he was taken to inspect a large, modern farm where cows were being milked *en masse* by electricity. 'I shall have a lot to tell my friends when I return to the Marshes,' he said. When Falih left London he went happily back to a small reed house on a small island completely surrounded by water.

Majid al Khalifah, the rheumatic old curmudgeon I had seen holding court in his tyrannical prime in 1953, may just be alive. He lived on in his Baghdad mansion after the revolution of 1958. He must be far older than Jasim bin Faris; about ninety, I suppose.

At the end of 1975, Amara took a long-considered decision

and moved his family to Baghdad. He had been sick off and on for years; he had had two operations for a stomach ailment that sounded nasty and which was visibly weakening him, even if it would not prove fatal. He had come to look so haggard I would not let him take up a paddle or a pole; and his friends agreed with that. Even cultivating his rice fields had evidently become too much of a burden. So he made the great move. Now he has his sons in school in Baghdad and a small house there. He earns his living as a watchman in one of the city's hospitals. His friends Farhan, Idan, Jabbar and Hasan bin Muhaisin tend his fields at Rufaiya and remember him. He visits them occasionally, and when I am with them they ask me to go and see him in Baghdad, which I do.

What is the future of the Marshes? I have indicated signs of progress. Doctors and nurses and clinics; schools; better access to the market towns and so more money; more cultivable land and so better food; lower taxes and no levies in kind: all these things the Madan have desired and required. For years governments expressed the intention of providing them.

Other, grander things have been in the planning stage at least since World War Two – flood control, irrigation systems, desalination schemes, land reclamation. Fine schemes like those are interdependent and they cannot be carried through overnight. Indeed they cannot be carried out at all if governments continually change, Ministers of Planning abruptly come and go, and priorities are inconstant. Iraq has money, oil, water. 'Give us ten years of peace and quiet', the planners and technicians say, 'and we shall work wonders.' If their prayer is granted, new dams in the north would divert water from the Euphrates and the Tigris to cultivate areas in north and central Iraq. The dams would reduce the volume of the waters annually replenishing the Marshes, and the Marsh region would naturally shrink. At the same time, new dams in the Amara area could turn the lower Tigris and Euphrates region into a vast and splendid rice-growing plain. If so, the future lands of the Beni Lam, the Albu Mohammed and the Muntafiq could rival the rich gardens of Sumerian Mesopotamia.

However the future develops, Iraq will need fish and reeds. Factories to process reeds into paper or fibre-board are to be erected on the edge of the Marsh not far from the little palm-shrouded town of Qurna for which across the centuries so many people fought. I hope for Madan, now that they have taken seriously to fishing, will still be appreciated for their incomparable prowess with boats and spears. It would be a pity if they were to abandon their ancestral homelands and become displaced peasants or factory-hands in anonymous overalls. It does not take long for proud rural peoples to go to seed in the amoral anarchy of towns: study the tragedy of the American Indians and the Indians of the Amazon basin.

Alcohol is a special danger. Nor is a townsman's health – despite his proximity to hospitals – necessarily better than a countryman's, even a Marsh Arab's. Uncurbed disease was the scourge of the Marshes in the old days. But now, with doctors, medicines and hospitals newly available, the Madan will not be automatically better off if they are shifted to small, stuffy concrete houses. Their reed houses have been developed down the centuries to keep out cold and heat: they are easily and cheaply built and easily moved, and are often a good deal cleaner than those in the overcrowded city housing estates. The Marsh houses have an undeserved reputation of squalor, usually propagated by those who have never spent any length of time in them.

The Marshes are alive. They are not a variation on Disneyland. Real people live and work in them. They can be visited. Today there are half-reed, half-brick tourist guest-houses at Qurna and anyone who stays in one can see how the Sumerians lived and moved on the face of these wild waters. The restless canoes flit about; the robed Marshmen are there, too busy to spend much time talking to strangers but certainly not hostile. The great *mudhifs*, representing a uniquely magnificent form of the world's architecture, crouch along the banks of the Euphrates like golden, hump-backed palaces. What you see today is very like the vision that captivated inquisitive George

Keppel, or competent Colonel Chesney, or 'Fulanain' all those
years ago.

Nor are the Marsh Arabs less fine-featured than they were,
or less mercurial. From all the excitements and excursions of
my years in the Marshes, I find it hard to pin down the memory
that most vividly conveys the essence of the people themselves.
It is curious. I found it perfectly expressed in a quite unexpected
place. In 1974, I stayed a night in the Government resthouse at
Qurna. I had with me a translation of Tolstoy's *The Cossacks*,
and because the next day was cold and wet I stayed indoors
and read it. There, in that incomparable story, a hunter spoke:
'Ah yes, that's the man I am! I'm a huntsman . . . I'll show you
everything. . . . Once I've found a track I knows the animal –
knows where he'll make to drink or roll about. Then I makes
meself a perch and sits there all night, watching. What's the
good of staying at home, anyway. . . ? 'Tis another thing altogether when you goes out at nightfall, selects a nice little place
for yourself, stamps down the reeds and there you sits and
waits like a good 'un. In the woods you knows all what's going
on. You looks up at the sky, the stars pass over and you can tell
from them how the time goes. You looks around you: there's
a rustling in the wood and you waits and you hears a crashing
and a boar comes out to roll in the mud. You listens to the
young eagles screeching, or the cocks in the village begin to
crow, or the geese will be honking: if you hears geese you know
it ain't midnight. And all these things I know. . . .' Put Tolstoy's
old Cossack alongside, say, Chethir and his son Shibil, and they
would sit together at ease. A Marsh Arab tribesman with his
sun-baked face and calloused hands, lying up in his *chabasha*
in the belly of the reeds, his net and spear in his *mashhuf*, and
his battered gun, dagger and sickle to hand, would know what
the Russian was talking about. When the soft, familiar stirrings
of the untamed life around them fall on their ears like the
well-loved sounds of an old song, Chethir and his friends enjoy,
without having to define it, an enviable oneness with their
world.

And now?

One day alone with young Shibil as he fished a lagoon, I said, 'Before I returned here, I thought I would never see the Marshes or any of you ever again. I thought you might all have vanished.'

He slapped his bare chest with his hand, sending a sharp echo round the reed verge.

'Vanished? We, Madan? Do I look as if I would ever disappear?'

He stood, laughing, in the prow of the canoe, brown and half-naked, his spear raised to strike down into the water.

And I thought: No, of course you don't.

But age overlaps age. The Marsh Arabs' way of life may, after all, be transformed before very long. I hope that they will be spared an abrupt uprooting, for that might kill something precious in them. All the same it may happen. So perhaps I should end with a prayer: That the descendants of the great Sumerians and of Khalid bin Walid's desert warriors may retain their immemorial clarity of spirit, whatever befalls them.

Let that blessing be on them now. And, if at last they are scattered, may it fall two-fold on their children's children in the centuries to come.

After which prayer from the heart, Ajram, if he heard of it, might murmur piously, '*Allah Karim* . . . God is gracious.' And then, grinning at me – because too much solemnity makes him fidgety – add in his rough and ready English accent, 'Damn and blast it!'

Bibliography

Arabian Sands, Wilfred Thesiger (Longman's, 1959) and *The Marsh Arabs* (Longman's, 1964).

Ancient Iraq, Georges Roux (Allen and Unwin, 1964).

Sumer, the Journal of Archaeology, published by the Directorate General of Antiquities, Baghdad, Vol. XXXI, Nos. 1 and 2, 1975.

Ancient Records of Assyria and Babylonia, Daniel David Luckenbill (2 Vols., University of Chicago Press, 1926 and 1927).

Travels Through Arabia and other Countries in the East, Carsten Niebuhr (Edinburgh, printed for R. Morison and Son, 1792).

Four Centuries of Modern Iraq, Stephen Hemsley Longrigg (Oxford University Press, 1925) and *Iraq, 1900–1950*) Oxford University Press, 1953).

Iraq, 1908–1921: A Political Study, Ghassan R. Attiyyah (Beirut, Arab Institute for Research and Publishing, 1973).

The Six Voyages of . . . Through Turkey into Persia and the East Indies, finished in the year 1670, Jean Baptiste Tavernier, made English by J. Phillips (Printed for R. L. and M. P. and to be sold by John Starkey . . . and Moses Pitt, 1678).

Journey from India towards England in the Year 1797, John Jackson (printed for T. Cadell, Jun., and W. Davies, by G. Woodfall, 1799).

A Voyage up the Persian Gulf . . . in 1817, Lieutenant William Heude (Longman [Hurst, Rees, Orme and Brown], 1819).

A Dweller in Mesopotamia, Donald Maxwell (John Lane, 1921).

The Expedition for the Survey of the Rivers Euphrates and Tigris . . . in . . . 1835, 1836, and 1837, General Francis Rawdon Chesney (Longmans Green and Co., 1850).

Travels in Koordistan, Mesopotamia, etc, James Baillie Fraser (Richard Bentley, 1840).

Personal Narrative of a Journey from India to England, Sir George Olaf Roas-Keppel (Henry Colburn, 1827, 2nd edition).

Loyalties: Mesopotamia, 1914–1917, Sir Arnold Talbot Wilson (Oxford University Press, 1930).

Alarms and Excursions in Arabia, Bertram Sidney Thomas (Allen and Unwin, 1931).

Haji Rikkan, Marsh Arab, 'Fulanain' (Chatto and Windus, 1927).

Arabian Days, Harry St John Bridger Philby (Robert Hale, 1948).

The Hashemite Kings, James Morris (Faber and Faber, 1959).

The Cossacks, Leo Tolstoy (Penguin, 1969, translated by Rosemary Edmonds).

Index